SUPERNATURAL TRANSPORTATION

Moving Through Space, Time and Dimension
For the Kingdom of Heaven

MICHAEL VAN VLYMEN

Ministry Resources

ISBN-13: 978-0692732250
ISBN-10: 069273225X

DEDICATION

I would like to dedicate this book to the Lord Jesus.

For in him we live, and move, and have our being.....

(Acts 17:28)

I would also like to dedicate this book to my wife Gordana and my kids, Matt and Angie, who have taken this very supernatural journey with me. God bless you.

CONTENTS

ACKNOWLEDGMENTS

I would like to acknowledge those who have helped me in this particular aspect of my Christian walk and experience. Those whose teachings and revelations have opened the door to me of the reality of supernatural transportation or translation by faith. Some of these people I know personally and consider dear friends, others are people whom I admire and have learned from but have not yet met.

Thank you Dr. Bruce Allen, Neville Johnson and Sadhu Sundar Selvaraj. I have embraced your teachings, prayerfully, and asked Holy Spirit to make this a reality for me.

I also thank the Lord that He has given me many awesome friends and others who have impacted my life who walk in the supernatural of God. Thank you to all of my friends who have so graciously helped me, come alongside me and spoken and sown into my life in so many ways. Thank you all!

I would also like to thank those of the cloud of witnesses and the angelic host who are always around to help us and to encourage us in the pursuit of His will.

Thank you all.

MICHAEL VAN VLYMEN

INTRODUCTION

How do I write an introduction for a book about moving supernaturally? I did not grow up believing that this was even a possibility, especially not for Christians! Even with all the biblical examples it was just ancient history.

But here I am, a man committed to Jesus Christ, and God has given me experiential revelation about this very thing!

This is one of the things that God is using me for and I am humbled, honored and excited to share these miraculous events with you. I will do my best to explain how these things began, how to see them develop and increase, and what I believe God is doing through them.

This book is a record of my personal journey in translation by faith or supernatural transportation or whatever name you may know it by. The previous book that I had the honor to work on concerning this subject was in fact "Translation by Faith" by Dr. Bruce D. Allen (and myself) and that book focused on how to begin to engage and then walk in this reality. This book is a record of the fruit that those engagements, steps of faith and exercises have brought.

I'm still learning and I pray that you will continue to learn and grow as well, all under the direction of Holy Spirit!

MICHAEL VAN VLYMEN

1

ADJUSTING TO THE SUPERNATURAL

I had been seriously and determinedly pursuing the supernatural things of God for quite a while before things started to shift and awareness and revelation came upon me. Those of you who know anything about me know that it was not a "cake walk." God didn't just hand me a special anointing or impartation to get things moving. I drew close to Him and He drew close to me. That was the dynamic.

After things began to happen, I had several confirming prophesies given to me within the span of about ten days from different Apostles and Prophets about the direction my life was going to take. It was like five different people reading me the same letter.

I know that sometimes we get a word and it's like "well...that could fit just about anyone." But these guys were telling me stuff that only God knew. Private conversations that I had had with the Lord. Things that I was doing and things that God had given me. The Lord definitely had my attention. But when you get words that challenge you, you may have to grow into them. Adjust to the idea or adjust to the supernatural shift. I'm still adjusting even now.

Full Disclosure

Ok.... As I dive into this subject I am going to have to give you a little background information. I am also going to have to repeat myself a little bit. Please be forgiving about that. Many have read a few of the testimonies I will share here in other books, or have heard me talk about them somewhere. I do this because I need to give a fuller picture here, especially in a book such as this one. My full journey.

Secondly, this book will be more about my personal journey and understanding of this phenomenon. I recently had the honor of helping Dr. Bruce Allen with the "Translation by Faith" book for Still Water's Walking in the Supernatural schools, and that book has a full measure of the steps of faith and activations that have born the fruit in my life that I will be talking about here. I feel that there is no need for me to repeat all of the activations and exercises here, but rather to share the fruit of doing them.

I would like anyone who reads this book will get the whole picture without having to read my testimonies in other books and then try to piece them together.

Step by Step

My first book about seeing had not even been written yet or even prophesied yet that I would write it, when I began to learn about going in the spirit.

A big part of my education was the It's Supernatural program and Gordana (my wife) and I rarely missed a show. As the

Lord was teaching me, He was also teaching me about pursuit of the things of the Kingdom. This is a very basic thing but it's also where a lot of people "miss it." We prayed the prayers, we stretched out our hands toward the TV, we did the prophetic activations. We did it all. We were hungry!

I think that to see a quick manifestation, one has to be *passionate* about this. This was my everything and there was nothing that held greater interest for me in the world. I believe that is the key. Unbridled desire!

I had been seeking and knocking and asking and still was not experiencing the spiritual manifestations I desired. I loved all the testimonies of God's power, I just really wanted to experience it too. I knew I was missing something somewhere. A key was available somewhere, I just needed to find it.

A Simple Instruction

My wife Gordana and I were seated in front of the television and ready to experience the supernatural when Brother Sid came on and asked this question...

"Can a man step through a door and find himself on the other side of the world?"

Then he continued... *"My guest was taught the secrets of supernatural travel and how you can do it too."*

I was interested. I was beyond interested. Have you ever been in that place where it looks like everything should be a go, yet nothing is happening? I was tired of that place. To be real honest I was inspired by all the great stories but I had not yet stepped into the supernatural. (at least not how I wanted to) Maybe it was my cessationist background, but all the instruction I had received so far seemed too ethereal, too vague. Things like "press in" or "hold on" or "break through". I wasn't making the connection.

3

Still yet, if you have ever seen Sid Roth's program you know he can get you stirred up. So I was excited. We watched as Brother Sid introduced Bruce Allen, a man who had been given a **mandate** by God to actually teach people translation by faith, or how to move around the Earth supernaturally for end times ministry.

I was totally on board from the start as he shared testimonies of visits to Heaven and meeting people he knew in the heavenly realms. As the program went on I was hoping that he would give a prayer of impartation or something to lay hold of. That's when Bruce gave a simple instruction of how to enter into the reality of translation by faith. It sounded so simple, maybe even too simple, but I've since learned that God does not make things complicated. Here is a short but accurate condensed version of what he said.

"Come before the Lord. Close your eyes and look.... Expect God to show you something and look for it..."

I had been looking and praying for some kind of tangible instruction for a long time. This was definitely that. Simple and to the point. I decided to try it and see what happens.

I didn't have the opportunity to try it that evening due to other obligations but had determined to try it the following day after everyone left the house. I wasn't nervous so much as excited. I had a feeling...

The Beginning

I made it to my prayer chair that morning, pretty much as soon as everyone left for the day. I was excited that I had an actual instruction that I could do from someone who walked in it! (translation by faith)

I settled back into my chair and got comfortable. I relaxed. I had the sense from listening the night before that I was not supposed to be anxious, but rather expectant. Relaxing was a way to keep anxiousness at bay. I closed my eyes, began looking and waited to see what would happen...

I waited ten minutes... then twenty... then thirty. At this point you could easily say "What am I doing?!"But I continued to wait. He was so certain that the Lord was going to show me something that I had to try. Thirty-five minutes...nothing...forty minutes...nothing. At about forty-five minutes I suddenly became aware that I was traveling at a very high rate of speed, right behind someone (an angel) while riding in an open vehicle of some kind.

But.....I was *also* seated in my prayer chair while perfectly still! After just a few seconds of this, it freaked me out. To experience both realms at the same time with full consciousness of both was more than I could handle. I jumped out of my chair!

I walked into the other room and let the memory play again as I tried to process it. I kept walking around, still feeling uncertain. "What am I doing?!" I repented from my fear. I told the Lord I was sorry for not trusting him to lead and protect me. I walked back to the chair. This time, I followed the exact same process but it was only about twenty minutes later that something began to happen. I began to hear all these loud and over the top sounds, bells and other things. I was hearing clearly sounds that were quite loud. But again, at the same time I knew that I was sitting in a completely quiet environment. I freaked out again.

I went through a similar time of reflection coupled with kicking myself. I knew that this was it. This was that key to get me experiencing some of those great things for myself. I had to go back to the chair until I could deal with it or at least muddle through it as I was learning.

I went back to the chair again. The third time I waited for quite a while. I'm don't remember how long it was but I know it was more than I had previously. This time nothing. Not even a hint that something *might* occur. I realized at that point I had blown it and I was a bit sad and feeling sorry for myself a little.

I went up to the bedroom and sat on my bed. I laid back on the bed and when my head hit the pillow, I said "Lord, I am so sorry. I'm sorry for being in fear over what you so freely gave to me." Instantly I found myself rocketing through the clouds and the stars. Then I was passing through clouds of stars and heavenly bodies. I was fully conscious and feeling more alive and awake than I had ever felt. My senses were heightened to the nth degree. I could see with incredible vision and clarity. I had a sense of knowing that I had never known before. My senses were all extremely heightened in every way. I ended up standing in a high heavenly place in the stars with the Lord Jesus. Although I did not see Him, I knew that He was with me and standing next to me.

After experiencing this exhilarating experience, I rocketed back to the Earth and was taken into the depths of the ocean. I stood on the bottom of the ocean and never had a fear or a sense that I needed to breathe or any such thing. I looked around in wonder. I was seeing all kinds of strange ocean life, creatures, fish and things I had no grid for. There was a white wall of some sort and it was alive. It looked like some kind of animal life big and soft like a jelly fish. There were hundreds of them and I was aware that I should ask before I touch, so I did and then I touched them. It was a wonder of wonders.

As I stood there in awe at the bottom of the ocean, the Lord Jesus spoke to me. He said *"See... I am with you even to the depths of the ocean."* And I realized that I did not have to be in fear.

If I go up to the heavens, you are there; if I make my bed in the depths, you are there. (Psalm 139:8)

The Lord himself had made it clear to me that I did not have to be fearful, He was with me. This event was the springboard or catalyst for me or in my life for moving supernaturally. The initial simple instructions that Bruce Allen gave that day became the foundation that the Lord had given me, and as I began to learn it expanded....a lot!

Even though I had experienced this, I still had no clue what the Lord was up to. I didn't see where this was heading at all. I was excited! That's all I knew and I was ready to engage again. I quickly got the book "Gazing into Glory" and read it through several times. It gave even further direction and I was able to glean even more. Looking back now I know beyond a doubt that this was where I was headed even from many years ago. God has been making preparations all along. You will see.

Time, Distance and the Supernatural

Even though for me this journey (the supernatural of God) started many years ago with my own deliverance and the sudden knowledge that Wow! God still does miracles after all! It has still been a learning process and continues to be. The major thing is being willing to allow God to show us things. It's funny how that works in most circumstances. God has written in His Word many promises and covenants and whether or not we benefit seems to be our own willingness to accept them. We can freely reject any gift or blessing as we have free will.

Accepting that God did the supernatural seems much, much easier for most if it happened a long, long, long time ago. *"In times past... God did thus and so"*... we hear the preacher deliver that message and it sounds so awesome and majestic that God *used* to do such amazing things. Most that even believe in the miraculous or think that it could have happened, leave themselves that comfortable distance.

Even in churches that don't believe in the manifest power of god today, they can still believe it to a degree if the recent miraculous event is still something from long ago. For instance ... Mrs. Johnson is a godly woman, she has served faithfully in the church now for seventy years. She tells a story that fifty years ago she thinks she saw an angel. Now everyone in church believes that it *could* be true. She a godly old saint, she lives her life for the Lord and the incident is from fifty years ago. Take the same woman and circumstances and bring the event closer.... Mrs. Johnson tells everyone that an angel showed up yesterday and helped her find her reading glasses. The same crowd would be more likely to not believe it.

Holy Spirit Brings Revelation

Of course, the Lord doesn't want his children to be unaware. So He brings revelation and also brings us along so that we can continue to gain even more. You can see this progression just by looking at those who claim the name "Christian" in general.

A very nice older couple stopped by to talk with me one day and mentioned to me that they were Christian. I said "Oh, you follow Jesus Christ too! " They looked as if I had cursed them. "We are not beggars!" the man spat at me and they turned and walked away. That is one end of the spectrum and the other end would be someone who literally believes what Jesus said when He said...

Very truly I tell you, whoever believes in me will do the works I have been doing, and they will do even greater things than these, because I am going to the Father. (John 14:12)

So... In my own journey it has been very much an ever increasing revelation... moving from Glory to Glory... and trying in rest to soak it all in. The reason that I mention the progression is because many have these issues or blockages that keep them from laying hold of God's promises and I want to make it clear that God will remove them and bring you into your promised land.

Having had that incredible instructional adventure with the Lord Himself, propelled me to a lifestyle of seeking His presence like I had never done before. As I talk about these things please be aware that I am not trying to impress anyone in any way. I am merely telling you what the process can look like and what it actually did look like for me. To seek God and see the miraculous is something that so many want (including me) but it very much helps to have some kind of instruction like the one that I received.

I speak to people every day who want the deep things of God. They want the strong meat. They want the supernatural and everything else God has for them. The truth is... it's yours. All of it belongs to you and God is not withholding any good thing from you. (Psalm 84:11) The only thing preventing most people is a small bit of teaching or revelation. Once the revelation comes, everything begins to fall into place. Then the only thing left to do is follow the instruction.

First Steps

My first steps into this phase of my journey were just a focused effort to repeat the experience that I had with the Lord. You hear people talk about the spiritual realm and it is hard to get the picture truly until you go or see for yourself. But now that I had a taste and an idea of how it happened I was determined to not just see it, but to live in that place. My intention was and is to walk in both realms with awareness. This was really the jumping off point for me. A big part of my entire journey started here. It's true that I had seen demons before, especially when interceding, but I was beginning a whole new thing now.

MICHAEL VAN VLYMEN

2

OUR IDENTITY

The things of God that I talk about today are so far removed from what I believed in the past it's sometimes hard to fathom. I knew that Jesus was God and the Son of God, Jesus was my savior and I knew about Jesus shedding His blood for our forgiveness of sin and our redemption. I knew a lot actually. My parents were pastors and missionaries for many years. I heard the sermons at home and at church many times. What I never knew however was that God had never changed.

All the things that made me fall in love with the Bible were always available all along and I never knew it. So now I am making up for lost time.

Jesus Christ the same yesterday, and today, and forever. (Hebrews 13:8)

We have to be in agreement with the Word if we are to walk in the supernatural things of God.

Manifest Sons

The Manifest Sons of God are not a special group of people that have memorized more Bible verses than others, they are those who walk in the spirit and power of Elijah.

It's doing the stuff. It's doing the stuff that people can't believe, won't believe, or don't want to believe that you're doing. I have trouble with it myself sometimes. It's allowing God to train you and stretch you. I mean really stretch you! The good news is that more and more people are laying down their agendas and reputations and just following Jesus no matter what. "Whatever you say Lord, I'm in."

If you thought that the gemstones, angel feathers and gold dust were hard to come to terms with, well... I think that those things are only the tip of the iceberg. In the lives of many friends, those things manifest daily. They don't mention it for the most part, because why would they? It's just a normal part of supernatural living for the manifest sons of God.

I was standing in the parking lot with a certain someone, who has become a friend, in front of the church where he was speaking one day. We were sharing testimonies about the awesome and incredible things that God was doing (including translations) and as we spoke, he just began to get covered in gold sparkles. The more he sang Jesus' praises the more he got doused! It is just wonderful to watch it happen and I love that kind of stuff! I do! I love the signs and wonders of God!

With Wisdom...Get Understanding

Make no mistake, it is very much a training process. You know someone who is "already there?" The Bible says we go from Glory to Glory. This revelation and walk is very much a living and breathing relationship with God. We can't walk in this with old wineskins. All the old understanding and revelation that we walk in may have to be set aside or left behind. Are you willing to lay down what had been wonderful and fruitful and now feels very comfortable, to embrace something unknown just because the Lord asks you to? I really hope so. God's plan is always far and away better than our plans.

Understanding is key because we can't really lay hold of something that we don't understand, at least in part. This very week I had to realize that even with everything that God has shown me, I still tend to qualify things by the natural realm. I really didn't want to admit that but it was true. It was really faulty understanding. We're supposed to know that the seen was created from the unseen. And knowing that we should realize that the unseen is more real and more tangible than the seen. But... I forget sometimes.

Wisdom is the principal thing; therefore get wisdom: and with all thy getting get understanding. (Proverbs 4:7)

One reason that this is so important is because as this supernatural transportation or translation by faith begins to manifest, you will learn many things in the spirit and by the Spirit. (1 Corinthians 2:13)

I know I'm not the only one with this particular issue, but the Lord is working it out. Many times when people ask me about my journeys or even my spiritual sight they will ask "did you see it *for real* or in your mind's eye or imagination?" Do you see what I'm saying here? *"Did you really* travel there or did you just go in spirit?" I was listening to Bruce Allen talk about this today and he says we have to get over the idea that our spirits are some wispy, cloud-like thing with no substance. Our spirits are tangibly real.

When I heard that, it reminded me of hearing Bob Jones say that seeing angels in your imagination is every bit as real as seeing them standing before you in the natural realm. We have to have this understanding of the spiritual realm. To walk as manifest sons we have to have an accurate understanding of this.... A true spiritual understanding and not with our intellect or reason. The things you learn, see or do in the spirit are quite real.

The mind governed by the flesh is death, but the mind governed by the Spirit is life and peace. (Romans 8:6)

We are not Defined by a Word

Over the last several years especially, I have become very aware of how much people love labels. *"Oh you're a _____? Then you believe this...."* I found this was true concerning basic terms like Christian or Charismatic, but is also very true about the name "manifest sons of God."

If you tell someone that you believe that scripture about the sons in Romans..

For the earnest expectation of the creature waiteth for the manifestation of the sons of God. (Romans 8:19)

...they will very possibly tell *you* what you believe. I have heard many people talk about the "heresy" of those who believe that scripture. Most likely they will also tack on some craziness as well, because to just say someone is delusional for believing a scripture doesn't seem much of an argument by itself. (except to unbelievers)

Why it Matters

Believing that we can and will be translated across the world, time and the heavens, pretty much says what side we fall on. If you decide in your heart and declare that you are a part of what God is doing now, you will be.

The belief that there is absolutely nothing that we can't do by His Spirit is necessary to *really* walk in this. (not that God can't give us sovereign experiences to encourage us) The greater realization we have the faster this will be manifest.

Many things were very challenging for me as God began to teach me about seeing and going. Many, many other lessons were intertwined in those lessons. Things that used to be considered allegory are now known realities.

The belief that we are supposed to and can heal the sick, raise the dead and cast out devils has been expanded a bit.

Heal the sick, raise the dead, cleanse those who have leprosy, drive out demons. Freely you have received; freely give. (Matthew 10:8)

Now, we are seeing that we are supposed to continue to grow in Christ and do the things He does. What does that mean? What does He do?

Very truly I tell you, whoever believes in me will do the works I have been doing, and they will do even greater things than these, because I am going to the Father. (John 14:12)

Herein is our love made perfect, that we may have boldness in the day of judgment: because as he is, so are we in this world. (1 John 4:17)

What kinds of things did Jesus do that we are aware of that might fit that bill? Feed people? Be kind to people? Yes, of course those things as well, but the kinds of things we are talking about are those things that have to be God. No other explanation is possible. When you do the "impossible" it has to be God and the glory is His.

Things like walking on water and walking through walls, walking through people or crowds of people, becoming invisible, instantly transporting to other places, multiplication of food, speaking to the weather and causing it to obey are all things that we know Jesus did. I will give a few scripture references, but if you don't know them you should probably look them up for yourself. Personal revelation is always better than second hand. Here they are...

Jesus walking on the water. (Matthew Ch. 14)
Jesus walking through walls. (John Ch. 20)
Jesus walking through people (Luke Ch. 4)
Jesus becoming invisible. (John Ch.8)

Breaking off the Yoke

I'm just going to say it. You were meant to do this. You were meant to do all those things that Jesus did and more, just like He told us to. Have the *audacity* to believe what Jesus said about you. Even in the face of opposition just refuse to believe anything contrary to what the Word tells us.

There is a religious framework that the majority of the church has been trapped in or framed by. The bondage of the comfortable and known concerning what is "proper" belief is exactly that...bondage. I deal with this from time to time as well. Every time we hear something that challenges us, we must remember to judge it by the Word and not fall back into the default religious position we may have been raised in. I know that by virtue of the fact that you are reading this book, this is not an obvious issue for you. I mention these things mainly because they are things that I have dealt with personally so I know that others will as well.

Every time we hear an objection to why something isn't or can't be God, we have to turn to the Word and the Spirit. The habit of depending upon men we have considered godly to tell us about God is not an option. We don't have to look too far to see that all the major denominations are handily making up their own "truth" now as they amble along, choosing what seems right to them instead of the Word.

A Prayer

Father, I come before your throne and I yield myself to you, body, soul and spirit. I thank you that your will, will be done in my life. Father let your holy fire burn away all of the deceptions and lies of the enemy from my being. Let all ungodly and religious frameworks around me that have manipulated and bound me in any way be destroyed Let every voice that speaks contrary to your word be silenced. Let my thoughts and understanding be by your Spirit and the mind of Christ be established in me.

You see what we are doing with this prayer. You can make a similar prayer according to the leading of Holy Spirit. All the religious practices that we may have done over the years actually sets in place spiritual ties, tethers and chains to bind us to those things. It makes it harder to follow the Spirit so we must break them off of us.

Hunger

If you want to move into the supernatural things of God, hunger and passion with bring you into the center of it. If you are going to pursue with passion, make it unbridled passion. Every godly person you know who walks in this is a source for you to receive greater things. I want to stress however the word **godly**.

You may be wondering why I have set such basic things at the front of this book. I have started to realize that it is sorely needed, maybe not for you but for many who will read this.

Every week I get messages and emails from those who are hungry for the supernatural. Because of the fact that I say that sometimes it takes time and commitment to walk in the supernatural things, I receive lots of instruction from people trying to "help me" by telling me easier ways to enter into it. For those who fit this bill, please don't fall into seeking revelation from those who don't know God. It doesn't matter how much they seem to know or what promises they make. The Holy Spirit is our guide. The Lord has given us many who are walking in this reality and those people openly share their lives and give *godly* instruction on how to walk in the supernatural according to the Word. Those are the people that we should be listening to.

But when he, the Spirit of truth, comes, he will guide you into all the truth. He will not speak on his own; he will speak only what he hears, and he will tell you what is yet to come. (John 16:13)

If you turn your passion to the Lord He will fulfill you. You will experience things you never even imagined. Even the journey is wonderful!

3
VENTURING OUT

Having had success by the instructions that I had followed and then gaining further revelation through the "Gazing into Glory" book. I began to pursue. Once you experience this, there is really nothing else that can satisfy you. The presence of the Lord, the atmosphere of His Kingdom is where you will desire to live once you have experienced it. I pursued His presence with a vengeance. (or at least I thought so)

I knew that my options during the day were limited. I have obligations just like everyone else and that left only nights for the most part to engage. My times of waiting on the Lord were both encouraging and frustrating. I would try to get into prayer and waiting as soon as everyone went to bed but sometimes that would be late and therefore I would start out already tired or sleepy. But the Lord had led me to the right time. At night you don't have the natural distraction as much and your focus is much more narrow because of that.

Sanctified Imagination

For probably a good month or more I engaged this completely in my imagination I believe. My process would be similar although led by the Spirit pretty much every time. I would worship, acknowledge Jesus as King and Lord, have a time of thanksgiving or really pray over things the Lord brought to mind and then lastly I would "wait on the Lord." I found that you really must be led of the Spirit because repeating a formula would be just like going back under religious bondage.

So sometimes I would worship for a half an hour and other times for hours. Sometimes I would be led to ask for cleansing and sanctification and again it could be minutes or hours. You have to be led by the Spirit.

The thing is that you can't grow impatient with this process. We have to remember that we are in the presence of God and enjoy that as well when we wait on God for anything.... Revelation, instruction or visitation will be forthcoming so let that inspire you but also enjoy the journey.

I began by quieting myself and then seeing myself (in my imagination) flying like superman to some foreign or distant place. I would try to make the event as real as possible because I understood that imagination was a powerful doorway. So I would "experience" flying through the roof of our house, flying across the sky, through the clouds or sometimes through the stars, feeling the wind on my face and the coolness of the air, going across the ocean and then landing in a place that looked foreign to me. I would then see myself either preaching the Gospel or praying for the sick or casting out demons or things like that. After a short time of doing this, I would fly back. All of this is my imagination.

I found that at first it was a bit difficult to do this for any length of time. It took a serious amount of effort to sustain this imagination with any semblance of reality.

Increasing the time spent took a little time. It got easier the more I would do it, so the time factor increased. I tried to set aside three hours per night to do this. Generally from about midnight to three a.m. Sometimes I didn't make it and other times I would lose track of time until I heard the alarm clock sound at six.

I just want to interject something here. In my own life I have learned as much by listening to friends tell me of their experience as I have anything else. If you look closely you can find little pieces of the puzzle that will be exactly what you need to reach that deeper place. Whether it's this book or any other. That's why I like to share my process.

Many times I would feel like I was not doing something correctly. The first time had yielded fruit in less than an hour and now I was waiting hours and not seeing anything to speak of. The Lord was also opening my eyes to a greater degree though at the same time. I would see the flashes of light, the room bathed in light, I would feel powerful presence come into the room. These were all things that were new to me. But it was enough to keep me moving forward.

For at least a month I kept up this routine, seeking God and believing Him to show me things. I had tasted it and I wanted it.

Exponential Passion

Sometimes we have a skewed sense of reality. In my own mind, I believed that I was pursuing God with all I had. And according to my understanding I probably was. All along this path I have had times where I cry out *"God show me! Show me what to do and how to pursue you and draw close to you!"* I had a vision once where I was standing before someone that I perceived to be a prophet and the angel who was with me said if I got in His presence I would be blessed. I wanted that so I took a step forward to be close to him. He took a step back. So I again took a step toward him and he again stepped back. The third time I said to myself "I'm going to lunge for him and be close to him and not give him time to move back." That third time when I lunged, he didn't even try to move away. He just stood there and I was drawn into his being. I then found myself back in my room trying to process what had just happened.

So even though I thought that I was doing all I could to pursue Him, there was more.

I have since learned of course that we are to be aware of His presence always. Just like Brother Lawrence talks about in the book "Practicing the Presence of God." My times of waiting were important. My times of prayer and praying in tongues during the day were important but.. the deeper connection is found in rest. Resting in His presence always. Always fixing our affections on Him Always being aware of Him and the atmosphere He brings. When we do this it becomes tangible.

My Second Journey

I was praying and worshipping one night, just normal stuff, praying over my family and needs and just looking for God to show me something. I went to bed and had been asleep for several hours when suddenly I found myself standing in a large hospital room with about a dozen beds in it. I was aware that I was in a poor nation. I was aware that all the children in the room were very ill, although I was not sure what the illness was. The room was semi-dark and there was a light shining in from the hospital hallway.

As I stood there I had a prompting to walk down the rows and lay hands on and heal each child. I was not led to pray for them but to heal them. This is one thing I have discovered about being in the spirit realm, you have a greater knowledge of who you are without the doubt and unbelief that might cause you to pray differently. So I went from bed to bed declaring "Be healed in Jesus' name." Over one of the children I was led to say "Be healed and delivered." After I touched each one, I found myself back home.

Many times I wondered about these experiences. Was it a very realistic kind of dream, or was it real? Things became more apparent as I experienced more. It was and is a learning process.

Dreams of the past came to mind. With many very realistic dreams I had to really understand that they may have actually been spiritual experiences and not just dreams.

Repeat the Process

I have heard numerous times from various people that once you engage something in the spiritual realm you have future access to it. This experience with the hospital visitation seemed the perfect occasion to test this out.

I began to revisit the experience in my imagination. Doing it often with great care taken to "experience" it as real, is a great key to laying hold of this.

Sanctification and Grace

Dr. Bruce Allen talks about this a lot. I have gleaned much from listening to his teaching and this subject is a very important one if you desire to walk in the supernatural. Sanctification of our thought life, memories and imagination gives us a clean slate to work with. If we have all kinds of random or unclean or distracting things floating through our head, you will not be focused on or have access to the things above.

I have been led many times to engage the sanctification process by faith. Asking God to sanctify me has brought me into some very interesting experiences. If there is any hold up or blockage in your life as you pursue the things of God, ask for and receive sanctification.

"Sanctify them in the truth; Your word is truth" (John 17:17)

By the which will we are sanctified through the offering of the body of Jesus Christ once for all. (Hebrews 10:10)

Provision has been made. From the Lord's side it's a done deal, however we have a free will. Do we desire to live holy and blameless before God? The modern grace message has done it's job to keep many from walking in the deep things of God. Believe me, I am all for God's grace. I need it. I have known people who are so thrilled to have a license to sin according to what they perceive as God's grace.

"Jesus has already done it all brother!" They exclaim! Don't fall into that trap. The word says that *the pure in heart* shall see God. (Matthew 5:8)

The whole "Let's see how close we can live to the world and still make it to Heaven " mentality is a dangerous place to be.

I like to make things like this very clear due to the fact that I have met so many people who desire to see the unseen and do the exploits of the Kingdom, but have fallen prey to the lie that they can have it both ways. We can absolutely have the deepest things of God. We can have more than we ever dreamed of, or we can have the lusts of the world.... But we can't have both. It breaks my heart sometimes because I see it so much.

We talked about this subject in the "Translation by Faith Workbook" also in greater detail. This is not optional. Because of the fact that imagination plays such a huge role, it has to be kept clean. I'm speaking of the purposes we are discussing here as well as the bigger picture.

So, in my sanctified imagination I was imagining ministry trips to various countries. Every night I would lift off out of my prayer chair and shoot through the roof, past the stars and a few clouds and be lowered into some place to minister the Gospel of Jesus Christ. It didn't take long (relatively speaking) until it started to become reality. The more I engaged, the clearer things became. I am not sure when the shift happened. I do keep journals but I was not recording all of my "training flights" due to the fact that I believed them to be only in my imagination at that point.

A Word About Imagination

This is a place that many people get hung up. Either people get weary waiting for a greater manifestation of the experience or they begin to believe that the imagined experience *is* the experience.

The imagination is the bridge between the soul and the spirit. Because we have lived so very long without allowing our spirit to be a part of who we are, we have a long bridge to cross sometimes. The more time and focus spent, the faster the process becomes. The bridge quickly gets shorter and before long becomes a door that you merely step through by faith. You won't have to guess when you make the connection when you finally step over that threshold from physical to spiritual. Even if you are physically wide awake when it happens it will seem as if you have been asleep and have only just woken up. Do not short change yourself in this part of the process. The saying that what you focus on you will connect with and then activation takes place is a true statement. Ask the Lord to give you wisdom concerning that statement and He will.

If any of you lacks wisdom, you should ask God, who gives generously to all without finding fault, and it will be given to you. (James 1:5)

...having the eyes of your hearts enlightened, that you may know what is the hope of his calling, and what are the riches of the glory of his inheritance in the saints, (Ephesians 1:18)

I was also desiring for greater clarity of spiritual sight at the same time. I had a few angels give me some helpful pointers and so I knew that continuous engagement with the spiritual realm was going to be a major key for me.

Being Single-Minded

I had a huge learning curve as I went. All the religious stuff that I had known I had to unlearn. Being single minded was one of those concepts that I had to relearn the right way.

Being single minded or not being double-minded is more than a mental ascent to a choice we have made. Its not deciding or flip flopping between yes and no so much (although it can be) as it is having everything about you in agreement concerning an issue or a question or not.

A double minded man is unstable in all his ways. (James 1:8)

Getting your body, soul and spirit all on the same page, desiring the same thing will bring a faster and more complete manifestation. This also brings along the thoughts, memories, imaginations, emotions, mind, will and various other doors or spiritual access points of our being. Be single minded of purpose with everything that you possess.

To Walk in Both Realms, You Have to Walk in Both Realms

I know it may sound strange to say it, but that is the reality. We make choices. Choose you this day who you will serve. Choose the spiritual realm and if you don't have that kind of passion ask God to give it to you.

My journey started out with passionate pursuit of God followed by seemingly random manifestations of God's presence and power. I was being taught of the Lord but I still had to walk it out. It's not like He told me something and then caused it to manifest immediately. The things that the Lord showed me, I began to engage them and do them by faith. For instance, He told me about the veils and had also shown them to me several times but the Lord didn't strip them away. I had to deal with them. I believe He did it this way so that I could share this process. The manifestations of those things were all over the map. I would go from powerful encounters with angels or transportations to nothing. Weeks of prayer and waiting on the Lord would seemingly yield little fruit. I did not realize at the time that the Lord was doing a greater work in me.

All the things I learned along the way I began to lay hold of.... By faith. All of the little "engagements" that I did were steps of faith that kept me focused on the spiritual realm.

To walk in the spiritual realm and I mean really walk in it you have to be engaged. It can't be the occasional curious look, it has to be purposeful. It may be a no brainer to you but many don't understand that. I have been told many times by people in ministry that they don't have time to pursue God the way I talk about it.

Walking in the Supernatural

This is a continuous thing. I need for my spirit man to function with the same or greater reality as my physical man. Everywhere I go, everything I do should be in both realms, or with awareness of both realms.

For me it has become a series of "engagements" that I have done until they became my normal day. From waking in the morning to look for the spiritual realm to speaking tongues before speaking English to scanning the spiritual atmosphere of the places I go, this is a picture of just being or becoming who we are. Awareness of our spirit all the time. Awareness of the presence of the Lord all the time. The more this is done, the more our spirit leads.

A Brief Overview of my Day

I know it's hard to read something like "Do this all the time" and feel like you're getting the whole picture. When I had the honor of helping Bruce Allen with the Translation by Faith Workbook, I asked how much stuff I could put in. He said put in everything the Lord tells you and everything you know will be helpful. So, I was able to lay out many of the things that the Lord has me doing throughout my day with staying engaged with the spiritual realm.

But, I still want to give you an idea here as well, without rehashing the material from the workbook.

I wake in the morning and as I wake, I lay still and try to make the transition from asleep to awake a slower process. I don't jump out of bed unless I'm running late. I look around my bedroom, sometimes with my eyes open and sometimes with them closed, or both. I'm looking for manifestations of the spiritual realm.

I tend to look in the north-west corner of the bedroom because there is quite often an angel that stands there and it is fairly easy to see him. Doing that "adjusts" my vision. Much like if you were to revisit a vision or experience in the realm of imagination. It brings a manifestation much easier.

As I get ready for work I pray and worship. I apply the blood over my family and household. It can take a half hour to an hour. I continue this process as I drive to work. I look continuously for the unseen and I am not disappointed. More often than not I see what I am actively looking for.

When I arrive at work I release the Kingdom over the place. I release the anointing and light. I keep an eye out for what is happening in the spirit. Lots of angels walking around throughout the day. Sometimes I can see them clearly, most of the time I see them faintly. Sometimes evil spirits make their presence known. I just rebuke them.

During the day, I play worship music and or messages from anointed ministers on You tube while I work. Many distractions come and sometimes it is a real effort to maintain my "space."

I lift people before the throne as I work. I pray over prayer requests and intercede. I try as much as I am able to experience being before the Throne as well as being in the physical realm.

At the end of my workday, or during any driving time, I use that time also as to be productive in the spirit. When I get home, my wife Gordana and I exchange stories of supernatural encounters or manifestations from throughout the day. (today one of the blessings was silver sparkles appearing in her mom's Bible)

In the evening as we fellowship and visit with family or friends, we are aware that we are all there in two realities.

At night of course I engage the Kingdom more directly through waiting on the Lord, prayer and worship all in a focused yet relaxed and intense manner. Sound confusing just a bit? Be intense in the spirit and let your physical man take a break. "Relax physical man, the spirit is taking over."

This is a very basic description of some of the things that I do. If we do these kinds of things at the leading of Holy Spirit, it will become normal to do the impossible. Your mind and flesh will not fight you near as much if you have already established these things in your imagination and in your spirit.

A Little Over the Top?

I know there are going to be a vast amount of people who read this and say "Yes. I do those kinds of things already." Then there will be those who have already begun. And then those who wish to begin. Don't let this dissuade you or overwhelm you. It is a natural process. It feels like work at first but your spirit is yearning for the proper order to be re-established in your being. Our spirit should lead under the direction of the Holy Spirit with our souls and bodies being under subjection. God will empower you for the task!

As we taste the fruit of the engagements or steps of faith, it really begins to be a joy and a pleasure.

Walking in translation or in translocation is walking in the spirit. It's like a powerful circle, moving from Glory to Glory.

4
Walks in the Spirit

Before I begin to share testimony of translations and transportations, I want to talk briefly about our right to see and go into the spiritual realm. Our rights have been granted to us by the Word himself. The Bible gives us ample permissions, encouragements and commands to go and do the things of the Kingdom. These are the scriptures that we all know and embrace, and the same scriptures that others try to present as allegory or metaphor.

So we fix our eyes not on what is seen, but on what is unseen, since what is seen is temporary, but what is unseen is eternal. (2 Corinthians 4:18)

One of my favorite verses. A very clear word to look at things unseen. It doesn't say we *should* do it, it says we *do* it!

Herein is our love made perfect, that we may have boldness in the day of judgment: because as he is, so are we in this world. (1 John 4:17)

Another very clear word. "As He is..." not "as He was", or "try to do the same kinds of things He did." Why do so many ministers have the gall to try and tell us what the Lord *really* meant to say. He could have said it any way He chose to....and did. He didn't have to say "As He is, so are we..." He could have said "Just try to be a good Christian" or whatever. People get so offended that we actually believe what God says.

I like to look at the testimonies of Phillip and Enoch and Elijah, Ezekiel and others and of Course our Lord Jesus as a model for how we should be walking in the supernatural. They all transported or translated or both. These testimonies are launching pads for those who are willing to engage them.

Invariably, I hear the argument against this even from Charismatic and Pentecostal ministers. It is a very sad thing and I believe it is because no one has thought of a way to try and control it yet. They have not figured that part out. Words of Knowledge... yes, we can set aside a special time to allow that just between the offering and the first hymn. "Thank you Holy Spirit, but we have an agenda to keep."

What I hear the most when people speak against supernatural transportation are things like *"This only happened to Phillip once and he wasn't seeking these kinds of things."* Or, *"Elijah was moved sovereignly by God, he wasn't looking for these kinds of experiences."*

Are you kidding me? These are people who lived for God! They knew their history. They knew that God was likely to do the impossible and I feel very comfortable saying that I believe that they wanted everything that God had for them. They didn't want the supernatural things of God? Really? Who told you that? I am more likely to believe that Phillip as well as others supernaturally transported all the time. The only reason that we don't have a detailed list of his transportation life is because we were given ample information to go on. To assume things did not happen because the Bible doesn't mention them is ridiculous. Even the Word says that if everything was written that Jesus did the whole world could not contain the books. (John 21:25)

The Lord gave us Matthew 10:8 They (we) were (are) expected to embrace the supernatural. It's who we are.

Around the House

One of the things that I tell people who desire to experience the realm of the spirit is to use their natural environment as a comfortable "launching pad.". Our homes, bathed in prayer and worship, anointed for God's purpose and filled with His presence is a perfect place to practice being who we are.

For most people this is a subject that we are desiring to experience the manifestation of. Even in having said that, it is also an area that is new ground for most of us. To step out in faith is easier if we are in a comfortable environment. A place where you already feel safe and feel God's presence will allow you to exercise boldness as you pursue Him.

It would seem that I discovered this by accident except that I don't believe in accidents in the life of a Christian. Especially in matters of pursuing God I don't believe we stumble into anything. God is orchestrating things to draw us deeper into His presence. He is fueling our passion for Him by giving us a strong desire to set aside the "joy" of this world and exchange it for joy unspeakable.

As I would go to my "prayer chair" at night after everyone in the house was asleep, I would focus on the Lord. I prayed and worshipped, meditated on the scriptures and just pictured being with Him. Sometimes I would get so relaxed I would fall asleep. Many other times I would pray all night.

It was comfortable. I felt secure just worshipping God and pressing into Him. No distractions or worries, no fears or doubts, just me and the Lord in communion.

Because I enjoy praying over my household, I would also do that before, during or after these times of waiting on God. I would walk through the house and anoint the windows and door posts I would also anoint various things that the Holy Spirit highlighted to me. I would walk through the entire house and pray over each and every room. For the rooms that had closed doors because people were asleep, I would extend my hands toward the room and pray.

I was learning some things about prayer and the Lord was teaching me to be diligent.

As I would pray and worship in the comfort of my prayer chair, if I felt myself getting sleepy I would just get up and walk through the house praying . It was and is a great way to continue and not fall asleep. I was finding that my soul or my body wanted to be satisfied even at the cost of missing a visitation from God. Being tired is a strong pull.

So I would get up and walk through the house and pray. Usually I would take the same path and do laps through the house. Sometimes for a long time. You have to understand it wasn't just about logging hours for my journal it was about praying *until* I connected with the heavenly, spiritual reality.

One evening as I was praying in my chair, I felt myself growing tired so I got up and began going through the house doing my nightly prayer covering. When I had gone through the whole house and made it back to my prayer chair, my body was still in it. I looked at my body sitting there in the chair and it threw me a bit. I had done my entire nightly prayer routine with the complete function and awareness of a tangible physical person even though I was in the spirit. But what I have come to understand is the tangible reality of the spiritual man or our spiritual part. So when Paul says

"...whether in the body or out of the body I don't know..." is so very true. (2 Corinthians 12:2) The spirit man is just as real as the physical...and more so.

Stepping into the Spirit

Once I learned that I could actually move into the spiritual realm like this, I began to do so on purpose. I would repeat what I had done in prayer, numerous times, recreating my time of prayer and waiting on God and looking for the manifestation of moving from the physical to the spiritual. I also began to learn to use my imagination to quicken the process.

How that began to happen was the teaching on the subject of "sanctified imagination" by my friend Dr. Bruce Allen. Many of the "exercises" and "steps of faith" that I do personally have been things that he shared with me early on or things that the Holy Spirit highlighted to me later from our previous conversations. The Lord uses us all to help others. Bear in mind that as God uses one person to help you, He will then use you to help someone else.

*I want to include an aside here on the fact that I mention people's names in my books. It is not in me to want you to be impressed by my mentioning people who are well known in ministry. I would be happy if it were the opposite. Be impressed with Jesus and let everyone else be a fellow laborer for the Kingdom, no matter who they are. The reason I do this is because like me, many of you will now look for the resources mentioned. If I give you names and topics or book titles, you will be able to find them easier and also take advantage of those resources. So be blessed and thank you.

The sanctified imagination can move you into the things of the Kingdom. The sanctified imagination is your spirit man getting involved. It is reality. Jesus said so when He discussed that lusting in our hearts (mind – imagination) is the same as having done it in the natural and physical realm.

But I tell you that anyone who looks at a woman lustfully has already committed adultery with her in his heart. (Matthew 5:28)

So realizing this to a degree, I began to actually "see" myself leaving my prayer chair in the spirit and walking around the house. I would "do" this prayer walk in my imagination throughout the house over and over. I walked through my house so many times in the natural with my eyes and senses seeing and feeling and smelling what it was like, it was fairly easy to reproduce this in my imagination.

I walked around as before and prayed. What began to happen was I began to experience actually going into the spirit for my prayer walks. I would go in the spirit and pray in the spirit. Then after I was done praying I would go back and rejoin my physical body.

To someone who is not looking at, or does not see the bigger picture it may seem frivolous to want to go in the spirit and pray in the spirit. "What is the point?" one might ask.

There are many reasons why God would bless this. One of the greatest is that we are called to be Christ-like.

...the one who says he abides in Him ought himself to walk in the same manner as He walked. (1 John 2:6)

Therefore be imitators of God, as beloved children; and walk in love, just as Christ also loved you and gave Himself up for us, an offering and a sacrifice to God as a fragrant aroma. (Ephesians 5:1-2)

Be imitators of me, just as I also am of Christ. 1 Cor. 11:1)
We are created to walk as He walks and do the things He does. I hope you already know that. Jesus said ...

Verily, verily, I say unto you, He that believeth on me, the works that I do shall he do also; and greater works than these shall he do; because I go unto my Father. (John 14:12)

Also, as with anything that we do, we normally would have to practice to make it a part of our lives. We don't start out as the one preaching to ten thousand but rather to one. As we learn, the Lord gives increase. I have found that in this particular thing, it is easier to lay hold of if we are learning in what we consider or believe to be a safe environment.

.....Till we all come in the unity of the faith, and of the knowledge of the Son of God, unto a perfect man, unto the measure of the stature of the fullness of Christ..... (Ephesians 4:13)

But strong meat belongeth to them that are of full age, even those who by reason of use have their senses exercised to discern both good and evil. (Hebrews 5:14)

The bigger picture here is learning to yield ourselves to God. Learning to move and listen and speak by the spirit of God so that we can move into maturity is God's intention for us. The only way that we can do the things that we are called to do is by His Spirit. Contending against horses is supernatural.

If you have run with the footmen, and they have wearied you, then how can you contend with horses? and if in the land of peace, in which you trusted, they wearied you, then how will you do in the jungle of the Jordan? (Jeremiah 12:5)

We must yield ourselves to do the things that our Bibles talk about. Forget what people say or think and be concerned with only what the Lord thinks. It is only going to get better... more extreme... more supernatural... are you ready?

I began to lay down on the floor to pray. I would go up to the bedroom and lay down on the floor beside the bed and I would pray. The floor being hard made is easier to stay awake to pray yet my reclined position allowed me to relax to a degree. Here I also began to get up in the middle of the night to do my prayer walks and many times would come back to the bedroom and see my body lying on the floor beside the bed.

The Spiritual Atmosphere

Being in the spirit even in your own home can be a learning experience. I noticed that in the spirit our house looked different than it does in the natural. There were some rooms, such as the rooms we pray in a lot, where the room seems alive and bright. Other rooms perhaps that were normally not used much had a much bleaker look and feel to them.

Also, if you are in the spirit you can see what's going on in the spirit in your home. I have seen many strange and wonderful things floating around the house from time to time. Numbers, shapes, lights and various other things fill the spiritual dimension around us. Do I always know what everything means? No. Of course not. This also is a learning process. As I encounter these types of things I ask the Lord for greater revelation.

I recall very well that on one occasion I was in the spirit and I was doing my nightly prayer walk. It was about three or four in the morning and I came upstairs to see my daughter Angie laying in the hallway floor next to our dog. Angie was in the spirit and her body was asleep in bed. At the time she had no awareness of what was going on. I told her she should go back to bed and lay down. She said *"I will Dad. I just want to lay here with Julia a little bit."* Her spirit was having a normal interaction and discussion with my spirit. The next day I found out that she wasn't even aware that this had happened. This is true for most people. Our spirits function in the spiritual realm with our physical beings having no conscious awareness of it.

Venturing Out

This very effective training ground was an awesome way for the Lord to teach me (us) the normalcy of being and going and praying and doing various other things "in the spirit."

You start to feel comfortable with being in the spiritual dimension. It's like we master one part and move to the next. Of course I had not really mastered this but I was adjusting so the Lord increased me. I began to venture out into the yard and around the house.

I basically did the exact same thing that I had done before (why fix it if it isn't broke) I had only changed locations. I would walk around the outside of the house in my imagination and eventually the shift happened and I would be in the spirit. I did notice something powerful concerning the manifestation of this however. If the imagination was something more extreme, such as imagining myself flying instead of walking or imagining myself standing on the roof to pray or something else out of the ordinary, the shift to the spiritual dimension seemed to happen faster.

I did love being in the spirit and being outside. I would pray sometimes early in the morning and go into the spirit and just take a walk outside to enjoy the morning in the spirit. I would feel the coolness of the air, the dampness of the dew and the sounds of nature coming to life. My senses were all there, only heightened. I could be in the coolness of the morning and feel it and enjoy it but I would never feel too cold no matter the temperature.

Because I was and am still adjusting in many ways, I did what many others have done in trying to take some kind of physical proof of having been in the spirit and going somewhere. I was looking for the inferior to give credibility to the superior. It just shows us how strong those earthly, carnal perceptions can be.

Moving Physical Things With Spiritual Hands

I was in the spirit one morning walking around in the backyard and patio area, when I got a *brilliant* idea. I decided that I would take some of the mulch chips from the flower bed and place them on the air conditioning unit and then come back outside in the morning with my physical body and see the mulch there. It would corroborate my "adventure" in the spirit that morning.

So that is exactly what I did. I grabbed a handful of mulch and placed it on the air conditioner. The problem was that when I came back outside in the morning it looked like about only half the amount of mulch that I had actually placed there. So that only left me with more doubts. I believe the Lord is not allowing this rampant having to prove himself to us, so to speak, because He wants us to realize that the spiritual is the superior realm and that we should think, and believe from that place of truth. Instead of constantly trying to prove the unseen by the seen.

But I did my prayer walks around our property in the spirit walking, flying, spinning (yes spinning) and various other ways. Sometimes the experiences would expand through seemingly no efforts of my own.

I would stand on top of our roof in the spirit and suddenly begin moving into the clouds and be catapulted into the stars. There would be angels around. Sometimes they would be set as what looked like rings of protection or rings of heavenly escorts. I like seeing the angels because it gives us a strong sense of God's love for us. The angels for the most part always seem happy for us and excited for what God is doing. Even those angels that seem more serious all the time give a strong sense that they are serious about being what God wants them to be for us. I have always felt blessed by seeing angels even including the angels that have rebuked me. It's always for our good.

Expanding My Territory

I don't consider the things that teach me or increase me to be happenstance. I believe that the things I experience as well as the things you experience are designed to bring us into our calling, fulfilling God's plan for our lives.

Although I am not going strictly by the timeline of events, this manifestation of moving supernaturally did have a progression that continually increased me and challenged me. All the while the Lord has also been giving me understanding to make me a bit more comfortable.

The Key of Intercession

I found that I did not have to always engage my imagination to launch me out into the spirit. Prayer or stillness or intercession many times was enough to do it. I found that particularly interceding for someone with concern or passion would very often move me to be where they were. I would go in the spirit to see that things were ok, or to see better how I might pray or even to do warfare at various times.

For instance, many times while praying for my children I would be transported in the spirit to where they were. This was one of the things that taught me the reality of what was happening. It would have been easy to dismiss things like this as realistic dreams, much like I did with encountering the spiritual dimension early on. However when you know the details of the places you have been, the conversations that you were there to hear and all the little things that in most people's reality you could not have known, you no longer have the option to dismiss these things. You know that God is indeed teaching you to move supernaturally.

A Family in my Prayers

There are many people that I have grown to love and be

concerned for and pray for. One family in particular, I felt the Lord was telling me how to pray for them. Something specific so that the things that were trying to afflict them would be driven away.

One night in prayer, I moved into the spiritual realm quite easily and naturally and because my thoughts were with them, soon I was standing in their yard. It was late in the evening, perhaps ten or ten-thirty and I felt compelled to walk around their house and release the presence of the Lord over that place. As I walked around the outside of their home, I could see them inside. The kids were having a sleepover and several other kids were in the TV room and they were all watching a movie.

The spiritual atmosphere was dense around that place. There was a heavy cloud in the spirit that was hard to walk through. I knew exactly what it was (as in the spirit we have a superior "knowing") and how I should pray.

As I mentioned I have also done this with my children. I have gone to see them while interceding for them and have recounted to them the things they were doing and the people they were talking to and what was being said. My family does not find this odd anymore. Once you begin to live in the supernatural of God, It becomes your "normal". But It does not seem to move unbelievers to believe any more than the signs and wonders do. I have realized that it doesn't matter how extreme the miracle is, people will not believe apart from the wooing of the Holy Spirit.

Intercession vs. Prayer

I have been moved supernaturally while in prayer but this did not happen until I had already been experiencing the phenomenon during intercession. I believe the passion and intensity played an important role in causing me to move towards the one that I was interceding for. The first clear example that I remember was a time that I was interceding for my son Matt. I had a knowing that I needed to lift him up and I did. I spent about four hours or more knelt down beside his bed at home, passionately praying for him. After four hours I found myself moving and wound up standing in his apartment.

Matt would always know when we were purposefully praying for him. Sometimes he would call at three or four in the morning and I would answer on the first ring. "Dad, I know you're praying for me" he would say. You can change things powerfully through prayer.

But I believe that if I had only prayed according to the way I understood prayer from my upbringing, I would not have moved anywhere.

Time is not so much the factor except in how it positions us to have what is already available. I know this because I have done the same for my daughter as I have done for my son on a couple of occasions and one time I don't think I prayed for much over a half hour before I was transported to where she was. Perhaps because I worried more over her, the intensity of my prayer was increased.

But time seems to take us to a place where we are more engaged. A five minute prayer can be powerful of course. In general, after ten or fifteen minutes you move to a deeper place. (at least that's the way it is for me) So when the Lord moved me to pray or intercede it caused a manifestation of supernatural transportation of some kind, many times. I have already explained why I believe God does this and there is Biblical precedent.

This enraged the king of Aram. He summoned his officers and demanded of them, "Tell me! Which of us is on the side of the king of Israel?" "None of us, my lord the king," said one of his officers, "but Elisha, the prophet who is in Israel, tells the king of Israel the very words you speak in your bedroom." (2 Kings 6:11-12)

Here we see that Elisha was able to move supernaturally to know the secrets of the king. I believe God wants us to know what is going on. I don't believe the children of God are meant to be at a disadvantage of any kind. The whole point of words of knowledge and words of wisdom, hearing God's voice and seeing what God is doing is so that we can act as true sons of God. Doing what He does.

5
SPIRIT LED ADVENTURES

Thank the Lord for biblical, supernatural experiences. Many times we wouldn't know what's available or what to ask for or pursue if God had not given us a direction. The Lord has given us many promises that as we seek Him he will guide us, teach us and empower us. If the Lord did not do this, it would be impossible to obey the scriptures. We cannot do what God tells us to do apart from His Spirit.

Howbeit when he, the Spirit of truth, is come, he will guide you into all truth: for he shall not speak of himself; but whatsoever he shall hear, that shall he speak: and he will shew you things to come. (John 16:13)

But ye shall receive power, after that the Holy Ghost is come upon you: and ye shall be witnesses unto me both in

Jerusalem, and in all Judaea, and in Samaria, and unto the uttermost part of the earth. (Acts 1:8)

One thing that I am fully aware of is that I am completely dependent upon the Lord. I first really got the revelation of this when I encountered unclean spirits and was a bit frightened by them. The Lord spoke to me within seconds and told me "I am with you. They would kill you if they could but they cannot because I am always with you." I learned that day that I have to depend upon the Lord. I have to just know my life is in His hands and I need to trust Him. *We need to trust Him.*

Another way that I am dependent upon the Lord is in direction in the things of the Spirit. Every day is a learning curve for me. When you go from just reading Bible verses to actually doing the things that the Bible speaks about, the Lord has to lead you. And indeed you want Him to. But we can have that confidence because of His promises.

"Which of you, if your son asks for bread, will give him a stone? Or if he asks for a fish, will give him a snake? If you, then, though you are evil, know how to give good gifts to your children, how much more will your Father in heaven give good gifts to those who ask him! (Matthew 7:9-11)

Sovereign Experiences

One of the most powerful experiences that I have ever had would in some ways fall under this heading. I wasn't asking for any kind of experience that day. I wasn't looking for one and at that time I had never experienced what I would consider the "fullness" of translation by faith or supernatural transportation. So I really was not even aware of how powerful this thing was.

But... it also was not God reaching down and doing something random and out of the blue to someone who was not wanting all that God had. No. my prayer is "Lord I want everything that you desire us to have and I want to walk in everything that you desire us to walk in". So I was and am totally on board with God doing anything and everything He wants to do with me and that includes every supernatural thing that is mentioned in the Word and everything else He wants to do.

So I was not in a passive, indifferent attitude toward the things of God. I was in prayer and seeking the Lord because I knew that He could be known and we can hear His voice just like He told us. I was passionate. So it was that at the very end of my prayer time that night / morning, I was propelled into a new phase in my training and experience.

On this day. I had prayed and worshipped through most of the night and didn't stop until a little after four a.m. I felt good. I remember getting up from my prayer chair and feeling refreshed and just thinking maybe I would go lay down for an hour before I had to get up for work. I stretched and walked into the kitchen and had a nice cool drink of water and eventually decided that I would step outside and take a breath of the morning air.

So I walked out through the garage and stepped out the side door by our garage. As I opened the door I could see the driveway and yard and trees etc., but when I stepped out I found myself in another place entirely.

I suddenly found myself standing in the front yard of a large church. The church was kind of behind me and I remember white trim and also bricks. I was facing towards the street and there was a man standing on the sidewalk in front of the church. He was a black man about my age with grey around the temples wearing nice but casual clothes. I knew that he was from the continent of Africa and I knew that his name was Joseph.

At the time, as I looked at Joseph I was not aware that I was not alone. The Lord was standing to my right and He spoke to me. He said "Take the money in your pocket and give it to Joseph." I hesitated and questioned the Lord. I was not aware that I had money but the Lord had put the money in my pocket. I reached in and took the money out and walked toward Joseph. "Here. This is for you." I said and then I turned and walked away. As I was walking away, I heard Joseph yell after me. "Hey! This will buy three containers of food!" He was very excited!

I believe I smiled and I walked away from him but I did not come back immediately. What happened next just goes to show you that even when God does the most incredibly supernatural thing, we (I) will still try to understand or prove it by the natural.

As I stood there in that church yard I had full awareness of what was going on. All my faculties were functioning in a normal but incredibly empowered state. I was not worried about getting home or thinking about any of the logistical issues with this "catching away". Even stranger than that, I was not even focused on the fact that the Lord had been there with me and had spoken to me! The only thing on my mind was finding out where I was so I could look it up on the internet when I got back home.

I saw two women talking with each other about thirty or forty feet away from me. They were also on one of the sidewalks in front of the church and so I walked toward them I interrupted them and asked if they could tell me something about Joseph. I figured that if they told me his last name or the name of his ministry or some other facts, it would give me something to go on. Their reaction to me was typical "prayer warrior type women at a prophetic conference" response.

One of the women said "Oh you find out all about him! He'll be here all week! But... let us pray for you!" Then they both launched into this incredibly anointed prayer and prophecy over me that blessed me and diverted my attention from trying to get information to investigate. They prophesied, among other things, visitations from the Lord Jesus and Enoch. They prayed for my spiritual sight and gifts.

When I came back home I was sitting in my prayer chair with what felt like waves of powerful electric currents running through my entire body and this lasted for about twenty minutes. I had no awareness of the transition between home and the church. It was just one step and I was there and one prayer and I was back.

Understanding by the Spirit

Now this is something that the Lord is still very much teaching me about. The reality of the spirit. The tangibility of the spirit man is a truth that we really need to lay hold of. I recently heard Dr. Bruce Allen teaching about this and it brought to mind several of the encounters and translations that I have had and I received a bit of understanding on it.

One thing that always amazed me early on was that I could be in the spirit and know that I was in the spirit and I could still interact with people (in the natural) and they could see me and touch me. I could also touch things and move things, pick things up and even drink water. I don't recall if I ever ate anything in the spirit but it would not surprise me.

In the past when I heard Paul talk about being in the spirit and not knowing if his body was also involved, I would think it was because it seemed so "real" to him. Now I realize it was because it is so real. The spirit can do everything the body can do and more. This explains (for me at least) why I can be in the spirit and not even know it for extended periods of time while I'm doing my prayer walks around the house.

I know a man in Christ who fourteen years ago was caught up to the third heaven. Whether it was in the body or out of the body I do not know--God knows. (2 Corinthians 12:2)

Yes, whether in the body or out of the body, both are tangibly real. I don't think Paul was confused about this at all. I think this is a little key that Paul (and the Lord) has given us for understanding what this is like and what it feels like.

And eating and drinking in the spirit is also biblical with biblical precedent covered in the book of Genesis.

The Lord appeared to Abraham near the great trees of Mamre while he was sitting at the entrance to his tent in the heat of the day. Abraham looked up and saw three men standing nearby. When he saw them, he hurried from the entrance of his tent to meet them and bowed low to the ground.

He said, "If I have found favor in your eyes, my lord, do not pass your servant by. Let a little water be brought, and then you may all wash your feet and rest under this tree. Let me get you something to eat, so you can be refreshed and then go on your way—now that you have come to your servant."

"Very well," they answered, "do as you say."

(Genesis 18:1-5)

As you begin to spend more time in the spirit, you will see that it is normal to function fully and completely and even at times to be unaware of whether you are in your body or out of it....just like Paul.

God Will Stretch You

I would say that almost all of my "sovereign" experiences are born out of times of prayer and waiting on God, worship and setting aside my agenda so I can be a part of His. Even for those times when I was not in prayer, my life in general was one of prayer and seeking God. I say this only because I am hoping that all who read these accounts will lay hold of these little hints and be launched themselves into adventure with God. This is another big reason that I don't buy that whole premise that Philip and Elisha, Elijah and Enoch as well as others 'were not seeking experiences from God". Why would they not be? They were sold out to God. What is written in the Bible that would cause someone to think that these very dedicated and passionate believers would not want everything that God had for them? It's in error that one would believe that.

I was seeking the Lord one evening when I suddenly found myself at an outdoor concert venue not too far from our house. There were many young people there at this concert who were very obviously drunk or stoned or both. I saw crowds of people walking in my direction and I felt I was supposed to walk in the other direction and so I did. At first I was trying to move and turn sideway to navigate my way through this crowd, but I realized that I was in fact walking through people. As I realized this, I didn't even try to avoid them, I just walked right through them. I could tell that many people were visibly upset at experiencing this and I would guess that they probably thought it was due to the alcohol or drugs. I walked through probably forty or fifty people and then found myself back at home. It was at the time one of the strangest things that I had experienced.

All the people in the synagogue were furious when they heard this. They got up, drove him out of the town, and took him to the brow of the hill on which the town was built, in order to throw him off the cliff. But he walked right through the crowd and went on his way. (Luke 4:28-30)

Ok... I understand why Jesus would walk through these people. His time had not yet come so He couldn't let them touch him. But why would God allow me to also experience this? I prayed about this and I believe God gave me an answer. Many times people get involved in things, drugs and drunkenness for example and the Lord being a good Father does whatever it takes to bring them around and rescue them.

I believe that the lord allowed this so that one or more people at that concert would have that supernatural experience of having someone walk through them and realize they should not be taking drugs or giving themselves to drunkenness. Why couldn't the Lord just have used an angel one might wonder... I believe He uses angels but He also uses us. He is bringing us into maturity and that means learning to be led by the Spirit and doing God's will. Regardless of what it is or what our comfort level is. We have to grow up.

Obviously I had not been seeking that experience. So in a way it was sovereign. But as I said also, I was seeking God and God is supernatural. When wie are willing God will use us in ways that challenge us and cause us to grow.

I believe that in the beginning of this journey, I experienced many more sovereign experiences including visitations as well as moving supernaturally than I do now. Now, I have a leading from the Holy Spirit to pray for someone or intercede. It is kind of like a word of knowledge or a word of wisdom. The Lord leads me to go and I start heading in that direction.

6

READY YOURSELF

You may read the title to this chapter and think that I'm about to lay some heavy stuff on you that will propel you into the Heavens. Well... in a way I am. I'm not going to share a bunch of complicated steps that you need to go through or difficult things to memorize or anything like that. I am going to share some of the simple things that the Lord has taught me along the way. These simple things will make it easier for you to lay hold of and walk in supernatural translation and transportation.

Experiential Knowledge

I have heard a handful of very anointed men and women of God speak on this subject many times now. They walk in the things that they teach. There are many others that also teach about this subject that do not walk in it. It does not matter how much a person knows about a subject. They can only impart what they possess. If a person gives you information that they have no experiential knowledge of they are only relaying "theories", even if the information is true. It will still be an unproven thing for them and even if they teach as if they know it is true, they don't.

Why this is important. If you know this works or that works you can say it with authority. If you only know what someone has told you, you cannot share it with the authority as one who walks in it. Therefore, if you are learning from such a person you may be spinning your wheels. I say this is important because to learn of these things you will most likely be breaking new ground. With all the material out there on this subject (and there is a lot) you don't want to spend months wasting your time, and you don't want to lay hold of anything weird. And weird can sometimes be very subtle.

God has raised up a handful of very biblically solid teachers who can help you learn to enter into this reality with complete confidence. Therefore you can be bold and move forward knowing that. The reason I say that here is the same reason that the book "Translation by Faith" contains the foundational teaching that it does. We can't allow ourselves to get sidetracked. Everything flows from our relationship with the Lord.

I have said that God has raised up a handful of people. There may be many more out there that I do not know about. However, I spent a lot of time looking into credible and biblical resources and many of those people are mentioned in my books. Having listened to hundreds of people who minister, I still have only seen a handful who teach this. Having said that, I also know that there are others who walk in this but don't feel led to teach it. So there you go.

As you position yourself to glean from those who are speaking and teaching about this, be wise.

By the Word and the Fruit

We are to judge by the Word of God. The things that we learn, especially those things that are extra-biblical, should line up with the Word. The reason that we say "line up with the Word" is because much of what we experience today is not written in the Bible. How can that be? It is just life as we know it. There are no references to any of the modern inventions that we enjoy today. If I say that in memorizing scripture you should listen to the scriptures you are learning on your mp3 player and recite them three times each, it would be foolish to say "where does it say to do that in the Bible?" We have to exercise judgment and wisdom.

Therefore, when you get an instruction, does it align with the nature of Christ? Does it line up with His character? Does it bring honor to the Lord? Does it speak of the Lord? Be led of the Spirit and you will be in good hands.

Also... Look at the fruit in the life of the one you are learning from. Do they lead people closer to the Lord? Are they humble? Do they really have a passion to see others walk in what they have or do they just want to talk about how special they are? Are they full of the Holy Spirit or are they full of themselves? I am throwing this out there from experience.

If you are getting ready to sign up for that conference and you notice that the Apostle / speaker is demanding to be addressed by his title and letting people know they should also bow slightly when they address him, save your money. Go to the one where the speaker is not above helping set up chairs before the meeting because it is not beneath them to serve. The people who truly carry the power of God have the heart of a servant. They are like Jesus. Apostles and Prophets are foundational offices. The low place. They are the support structure and they know it and wouldn't have it any other way.

Two of the most powerful displays of gifting that I have ever seen, came from two pastors from the same church in Western Australia. A day apart each one spoke into my life having never met me before. They both told me very specific things and even knew of my actions and dreams and "secret" communication I had with the Lord. You know what they had in common? Humility. Both had the heart of a servant. One pastor was helping to park cars before the service and the other was always making himself available to pick up and drive around the visiting ministers any hour of the day or night. So look for these types of things.

The people that I learn from whether from their materials or through direct communication have this maturity in Christ. They know who they are so they don't need to posture or pose in any way. They have the Father's heart. They sow into people. They bless people. They encourage. They do everything that they can to make sure we "get it".

Simplicity

You may really need to read this part or maybe you don't. But I have seen that many, many people do not lay hold of translation or transportation because they over complicate the process. I understand that there is a lot to learn on many levels when you are talking about walking in the supernatural things of God. I know that. But there is a process. We don't study Trig before we have mastered basic addition and subtraction. We don't learn the workouts of professional athletes our first day at the gym.

If you really want to do the stuff, you have to take a simple step and learn to lay hold of it before you try to "learn" and move on. You cannot move on to point b or c or q until you have taken hold of point a.

Let me give you a couple of real world examples....

When I first began pursuing the supernatural things of God I listened to everybody I could find. I prayed and decreed and learned things and still I was missing something. Now even though I had to go back and learn or relearn some things later, the simple direction that powerfully kicked off my journey was *the simple instruction* I gave you in an earlier chapter. Once I knew the power of that and really laid hold of it, it was manifesting in my life. Then I began to learn and lay hold of more.

I had a similar experience with other materials as well. I was listening to a lot of stuff. With some, I was excited and confused at the same time. Can anybody else relate to that? I'm going to share a secret to really laying hold of what you study.

I was complaining to the Lord one day as I have been known to do from time to time about the fact that I was not understanding many things. Particularly a couple teachers. The Lord told me "It's very simple." I said "o.k. Lord... what is it? " The Lord told me that some are using words that I did not truly know the meaning of and the were talking about spiritual realities that I had not studied or even looked into. To make His point clear, He asked me the definition of the word "mandate." Although I had a general idea, I truly didn't know the correct definition.

So... just like in math class, if you miss a day or a week or even just a part of the equation it is almost if not impossible to solve it. I believe that although he says it in a funny way, this is why he always says "get the cd!" because we will not get it and understand it in one listening. Also, what I have come to see through what the Lord taught me about this is that just like Bruce, others also give the simple instructions that are meant to cause these things to manifest in our lives.

Case in point... I will just mention two examples. In a teaching about the separation of our soul and spirit, there was a very specific and simple instruction to carry out. It was explained completely and slowly several times. I learned how important and powerful this was to the speaker and for us as well. The process was laid out and explained that we had to do this every day for about thirty days. I believed spent some serious time gaining the manifestation of the separation of spirit and soul. That's one.

The second is where people stand and take a step forward (by faith) into the spiritual realm. Take a step forward in and then a step backward out. Very simple. There are more explanations about this and many have talked about how important this was as a step of faith.

I mention these two things because they are both very powerful and very simple. Anyone can do this. I have spoken to many people who are trying to access heavenly places or interact with angels or do various other things. When I ask if they have done some of these simple steps that he has explained, I am finding that many have not because they want to jump ahead. I will just say that those who are trying to bypass the basics will not get very far. I encourage you to know that you can step into some completely otherworldly experiences in God just by really doing due diligence to the foundational things. Then you can increase from there.

If you will take one simple thing at a time and really go for it, you will be completely undone by what happens. This has been a common problem for so many people that I really want to encourage everyone to go back to the basics if you are not where you want to be. Don't continue to be frustrated about not entering into the full measure God has for you. Go back and focus on these things and allow God to move through them.

There will come a time for you to go deeper and for understanding to increase. You will learn about heavenly places and dimensions, angels and hierarchy but for now just get through the door. Once you are in and you know what it feels like and looks like, you know how the transition feels and the steps leading up to it, you are positioned to be increased.

Be Yielded

One thing that I learned early on in these types of experiences was that we have to be yielded to the Holy Spirit. Don't try to go into the spiritual realm with any agenda of your own. Be led of the Spirit.

Many times I would purpose in my heart that when I would go into the spirit, I would find a place to kneel and I would pray in tongues. It sounds like a "God honoring" plan right? Well, that was my intention but every time I would try that I would get sucked back into the natural realm. If I had a natural thought for direction while in the spirit, I would be brought out by that means also.

What I found out for me at least, I had to be led of the Spirit even in the moment. I would wait and not do anything until the Lord would lead me in some way. I would recognize that He was doing something and I would yield to it. Then I would be taken into adventures in God. Even doing good things is not enough. We have to do what God is doing.

The scripture that talks about Jesus only doing what He sees the Father do is important for us also.

Then answered Jesus and said unto them, Verily, verily, I say unto you, The Son can do nothing of himself, but what he seeth the Father do: for what things soever he doeth, these also doeth the Son likewise. (John 5:19)

Start Moving in the Right Direction

How do we do this? We are learning how to do this but there are people for whom this is an everyday or every week occurrence. Preparation, although somewhat limited is still very possible. When you are looking to learn to heal the sick, immerse yourself in healing testimonies. Likewise when you are learning to see in the spiritual dimension, testimonies of those who see clearly will propel you in that direction.

When it comes to supernatural transportation or translation, soak up every credible testimony that you can find. Make this the backdrop or soundtrack of your life for a season at least until it really begins to manifest in your life.

In addition to listening to modern day testimonies, read every scripture that talks about moving supernaturally and meditate on those scriptures. Even if you are not fully able to give yourself to this process at least make sure that you are replaying these testimonies in your imagination as you lay down to sleep. Your spirit is very willing and you will find out just how willing you really are.

Testimonies are very powerful and you can take hold of them to open doors and blessing etc. in your own life.

Two Realms, Two Worlds

You can absolutely live in the spiritual and natural realms with conscious awareness of both. If that is your desire you can have it. Not only can you have it, God will give you the grace to experience this as normal. There will be an adjustment period but as you grow, you will become comfortable being who you were created to be.

The one thing that you can't do is walk in both *worlds*. The scripture says ....

And if it seem evil unto you to serve the LORD, choose you this day whom ye will serve; whether the gods which your fathers served that were on the other side of the flood, or the gods of the Amorites, in whose land ye dwell: but as for me and my house, we will serve the LORD. (Joshua 24:15)

You might be thinking "Mike, if I wasn't seeking to serve God I certainly wouldn't be reading a book like this." And to be fair, that is probably true. But what I'm saying is that we have to be aware. We have to be *really* aware. Many times the things that trip us up are very subtle.

The enemy wants to keep us from walking in the power of God. He wants to keep us out of the supernatural. There are so many Christians across the Earth who really have this wrong. So many Christians live in fear of the supernatural, fear of the enemy and fear of spiritual things. God has not given us a spirit of fear, so where does all that fear come from?

The enemy wants to keep Christians out of the supernatural. Once a believer finds out who they really are in Christ, all bets are off. Once the blinders come off and we see that we are literally seated in authority in the spiritual and heavenly realms we act and pray with boldness.

So the enemy will be very subtle many times to keep us from our inheritance.

The Lord had to teach me some hard lessons about this several years ago. I had to be told and reminded several times of "what fellowship has darkness with light?" I had friends in my life that I felt I could have fellowship with. The reasons that I *could not* were subtle... *almost* accidental. The Lord told me several times in a kind and patient manner to cut out "hanging out" with several people. I did not obey.

Because the Lord is merciful and He wants to keep us safe and on the right path, He told me again in some powerful dreams. I kind of listened, but in reality I did not.

Ok... So what was the issue that I couldn't see? I had people in my life who were believers but living "sloppy" lives. They were relying heavily on God's grace so they could pursue questionable things and I was turning a blind eye. But it was subtle. We would talk about spiritual things when we got together. And probably only two percent of our conversation was unpleasing to God. I felt that because I was not the one doing and saying wrong things, it was ok. I considered myself a merciful witness. I was deceiving myself. The enemy was using certain people to bring defilement into my home.

Can it really be that bad if someone tells you an off color joke or says or does something ungodly in your presence? After all, it wasn't you doing it.

It doesn't take much. The fact that the Lord said it was important should have made it a done deal. But not only was I allowing this influence in my home, I was in disobedience to the Lord. How is the Lord going to pour His power into a disobedient vessel? It's not going to happen.

Guard your life jealously. Guard your home and family and atmosphere jealously. Guard every door, access point and portal into your life. Make it a priority.

For the sake of clarity I want to say that there are people around our lives the we love and have to be around. There are family members who are either unsaved or new believers and co-workers and people at church that want to say hi and things like that. That is all vastly different from the type of fellowship I'm talking about. Be led of the Spirit and obedient to God's voice.

The reasons that I mention seemingly random and unrelated things is because they are neither random nor unrelated. It would greatly discourage you to pursue the deep things of God for a couple of months or years only to realize that the reason you have missed it is because of something simple that I could have shared with you. I will just share all I feel compelled to and you can decide what is important for you.

Just examine your life in an ongoing manner and ask the Lord to reveal anything that is displeasing to Him. He will do it. He will keep you on the right path if you listen to His voice.

7

MOVING ACROSS THE EARTH

It wasn't long after I had my initial trip into the heavens with the Lord Jesus that I began to have other types of trips. Having really pursued this with a vengeance I realized that the more I gave myself to the Lord for this purpose, the more it happened. Perhaps a little more than a month had gone by and I began to go everywhere. Well... at least it seemed that way.

I already gave the testimony of being sent to give a man named Joseph money for his ministry. But the Lord had far more in mind and I was excited to be a part.

Some of the most intense experiences I have had have been when the Lord has taken me to other countries to do His will. Here are a few of those trips. I have mentioned a few of these experiences in other books but please don't be disappointed. I want to give as full a record as I can about this subject in this book.

Buongiorno Italy

It was nighttime when I left my prayer chair and wound up standing in a kind of intersection where two narrow streets intersected somewhere in Italy. I would place the time somewhere around mid-morning there. The street was filled with lots of people going about their day. The buildings were stone, some colored brightly and although I was in the street, there was no automobile traffic for some reason. I'm guessing it may have been a promenade of some sort.

I was standing on one side of the street and on the other side there was a crowd of people (twenty perhaps) standing in a group over what appeared to be a young boy laying in the street. I felt compelled to go to him.

As this was happening, I did not have the awareness this time that "this is why I am here". The situation took my full attention and I did not give a second thought to the fact that I had translated there at that point. I walked over to the boy and I knew he was dead and that the man who was weeping over him was his father. I told the man "I'm going to pray for your son and the Lord is going to raise him up." The man in his grief got very angry at me and started yelling at me. "He's dead!" he yelled as well as a few other things.

Within seconds the entire crowd was yelling at me angrily. In the natural, I might have been completely shaken by this. In the spirit realm however, there was absolutely no doubt or fear whatsoever. I knew what God was going to do whether anyone thought so or not. I have found this to be the common thing about being in the spiritual realm. You *really* know who you are.

No one stopped me as I knelt to touched the boy and told

him to wake up. Within seconds the boy opened his eyes and I told the man "take your son and go home." I don't know why I said that, I was just led by the spirit to say it. At that point the crowd became silent and they all just stared at me. I don't remember preaching the gospel or giving testimony of what had happened. I stood there and looked back at the crowd in silence. The next thing I knew, I was back home.

The Next Day

The very next day during my prayer time I suddenly found myself standing in front of an old blue wooden door in a similar type setting as the night before. What do you do when you are standing in front of a door? Knock! So I knocked on the door and who should answer but the man whose son I had prayed for the previous day!

I very quickly explained to the man what had happened and why God had raised his son back to life. I shared the gospel and the family gave their hearts to the Lord. I never went beyond their front step. I then blessed them and turned and walked away. Again, at this point the next thing I knew I was back home.

*On a practical note... When I have spoken to people in other languages it very often feels as if I am speaking English and it's coming out as something else. It feels very natural and normal.

The Russian Elevator Repairman

This trip also happened during my prayer time at night. I suddenly found myself standing in the hallway of a large apartment building. I am not sure what country it was but it was a big building so it must have been a city. Not far from where I stood in the hall, there were was an elevator and middle aged man wearing a gray uniform of some type was standing on a ladder and working on it.

I walked over to him and I began telling him that Jesus loved him and He wanted to give him good things. I told him that several times and he actually started to get very angry with me. I was also led to touch his arm as I told him the Lord loved him. I think that he sensed that I was doing something to him and began to come down off the ladder. Because of the look on his face, for a moment I thought he might hit me. But suddenly as he came off the ladder, he broke down and became very emotional. At that point I just shared the gospel and the man gave his heart to the Lord. It was a very, very neat thing! Also, during the course of talking to the man (we were speaking in Russian) he used a word that I did not know. It was the word "razresheniye".

It had been a long time since I studied Russian and I don't use it enough to be fluent and I told him that I didn't know that word. He spoke some English and told me the word meant "understanding". After I got back, I went to the computer and discovered that it indeed meant understanding. The Lord could have easily allowed me to have an "understanding" of that word, but I believe the Lord allows little glitches like this so you will know that He is really doing this. He wants us to be aware of that fact.

I also had some understanding that the man's wife had been praying for him and the Lord was answering her prayer.

A Quick Stop at the Diner

I was translated one day to a small diner somewhere in a small town somewhere in the United States. The diner looked like a throwback to another era. There were round stools at the counter and only about five or six booths. I don't recall the diner being real busy but there were probably eight or ten people in there.

At the end of one of the booths was a man about thirty years old with dark hair in a wheelchair. He had some kind of muscle disease where his limbs were twisted and held in place and he had no control over them. He was completely bound. I mean in the spirit also he was completely bound. In the spiritual realm I saw many black ropes around him tying him into that weird position he was in. The ropes were the spiritual reason for the physical manifestation. I walked over to the man and told him "I'm here to pray for you." And just like what happened in Italy, as if on cue the people in the diner began mocking me and getting angry. Telling me to leave him alone. It seems like whether in the natural or in the spirit, when you minister you still have to deal with this.

I laid my hand on his chest and his body began jerking and moving and twisting violently. This continued for less than a minute and then the man then slumped over in the wheelchair appearing to be unconscious. But now his body was relaxed and there were no ropes around him anymore. When I walked out of the diner the man was still slumped over in the chair. I left him like that. I don't know what transpired after that obviously.

When I walked out of the diner I saw a woman standing by a fountain across the street from the diner. I didn't know her name or anything about her except for the fact that her knee was messed up and she was in pain. I walked over to her and told her that God had shown me that she was in pain from her knee and I was supposed to pray for her.

She allowed me to pray. I lightly and barely touched her knee cap and she was healed. Again, the transition back to the house had escaped me. I just found myself home.

Protecting Kids in Central America

As if these types of things were not already a bit strange (especially at first). This particular event was just a little bit more strange.

This particular day I moved from being asleep in my bed to riding a bicycle down a hill on a street in Central America with full conscious awareness of what I was doing. There were two shady looking men who were hanging around the area that I was sent to. They acted as if they were going to try something against me but I did not have or show fear, so they didn't pursue me. I rode the bicycle down to the bottom of the street and turned into a little driveway where there was a run-down, two-story house.

I was led to climb the stairs and go and stand on the front porch of the second story. I was not told why, but I did know that there were two small kids in the house by themselves. I stood there for a while until I felt like it was time to go and then I rode away on the bicycle. I never had any more knowledge about the situation but was happy to have been used anyway.

I had a sense that perhaps I was just there to stand in the way of someone trying to harm those kids. Once the danger had passed, I was brought back.

A Hospital Visitation

I have been sent to hospitals several times. That makes sense as they have sick people there we can pray for. But I walked into a room where a man was standing over his son who was very sick and the boy had some yellow thing on his face. A breathing apparatus I believe. I asked the father what was wrong and he told me his son had a problem with his throat, but wouldn't tell me any more.

I explained to the dad that God could heal his son and the man told me that he was agnostic and didn't believe or want me to pray. I finally convinced him and when I was about to pray the boy said "No."

So I told him "Ok... I won't pray, I will just release God's power. I held my hand out toward him and I could feel the power begin to manifest. When it had manifested I pushed it toward him. I did this three times and the power of God physically moved him all three times.

After that, I talked with the family and told them what God is doing on the earth and that they could also be a part of it. Just before I left the man thanked me and was genuinely appreciative. I gave him a hug and then I was back home.

The hospital visits that I have done have all been awesome. I experienced it the first time Without asking for it. After the first time, I used the memory of the experience to ask for further hospital visits where the Lord would use me to pray.

Meetings, Crusades and Ministry Trips

One thing that the Lord has allowed me to experience has been to attend at least in part different meetings put on by various ministries.

I was once translated to the middle east to a crusade that Benny Hinn was doing and I got to watch Pastor Benny give a word of knowledge to someone about getting a job working for the king and that he would have favor with the king. It was very cool!

I also have been blessed to attend a conference in the spirit and sat in the front row. I don't remember a lot about the message now but it was significant for the time I was in.

Once I was translated to Brazil to help a minister who was on a mission trip there. I was completely in the spirit and there were four very big angels who were with me that I saw and interacted with. I was giving the driver directions of how to get where he needed to go and then I talked to the hotel staff and cleared up a problem concerning their rooms. At one point, the ministry team was going out to eat, and I said that I wanted to stay behind. . One of the angels stayed back with me and the others went with the team. I came back right after.

A Nice Place to Take a Walk

One of the places that I like to go to minister is a place on the other side of the world where there is this awesome street where no cars are allowed and people walk and shop and drink coffee at little cafes. I got in the habit of picturing this place in my imagination and walking through the area and praying for people. It wasn't too many times before it became a reality and I would just walk around and seemingly randomly find people to pray for. I remember praying for a young boys leg one day and it caused some excitement when God healed him.

I also went back to this place one day for another reason that I will share in another section.

8

TRAVELING UNSEEN

Traveling unseen is an awesome thing. You get to see what is really going on behind the scenes or you can pray or learn things without the physical interaction.

I think of the story of Elisha listening to the King's plans in his bedchamber in second Kings.

...This enraged the king of Aram. He summoned his officers and demanded of them, "Tell me! Which of us is on the side of the king of Israel?" "None of us, my lord the king," said one of his officers, "but Elisha, the prophet who is in Israel, tells the king of Israel the very words you speak in your bedroom." (2 Kings 6:11-12)

God has many different reasons for wanting you to travel unseen in the spiritual realms. Just like Elisha.

The Reality and the Proof

One of the things that I first was challenged by was the fact that I had no grid for much of what God was doing. I know that these things are talked about in the Bible, but I had never been taught these things growing up. Indeed I had been taught just the opposite like most people.

So even though my encounters and experiences were completely interactive and with full conscious awareness, I would still consider them to be "only" dreams. That was as supernatural as I could go at the time. What the Lord did was show me through traveling unseen that I was indeed going in reality. It was not a dream but it was reality in the spiritual dimension.

Checking on the Kids

I learned quite quickly by passionately praying for my children that I could be translated to where they were. I could see where they were, who they were with and what they were doing.

When my son Matt was living in Bloomington, Indiana going to school, there were several times that I spent the night in all night prayer vigils for him. The Lord in his mercy would allow me to translate to Matt's apartment and check in on him. I would be standing in the apartment with Matt and his friends and I would observe them and listen to the things they were talking about. The next day I would tell Matthew what had happened and I would relay who was with him and what everyone was doing and talking about.

In our household this is no longer weird but just a normal part of being a child of God.

Also with my daughter Angie the Lord allowed (allows) this as well. It is a real blessing to be able to go and make sure your kids are ok.

Lord I Need to Know

Sometimes people have dire needs and we really need to know how to pray. I had a prayer request from a family who was at the end of their rope. Sometimes, just like Elisha, the Lord will take you unseen so you will know exactly how to pray.

A young couple was asking for prayer over and over for their young son. Suddenly, for seemingly no reason he had become violent and was doing mean things to the other smaller kids at school. This had seemed to come out of nowhere and the parents were at their wits end. The parents had taken him to specialists and others and nothing was helping. By the time I was asked to pray, it had been going on for almost a year.

I had prayed for him for a couple weeks and there was no change. I told the Lord, "Lord, you have to show me what's going on. What is tormenting that child so that he acts that way?" Be sure of one thing. If you ask, you will receive.

This is why we need to move in the supernatural of God....

After praying that prayer, the Lord took me in the spirit to show me what was going on in this boy's life. When no one else was around, an older relative was tormenting this young boy. Terrorizing him so wickedly and savagely that the boy was completely traumatized. The Lord actually let me watch this. The boy had no one he could tell (for fear) and no hope. This fear and frustration and hopelessness was manifesting by him trying to do something to find help in some way.

I witnessed this in the unseen realm and I have to be honest and tell you I felt sick watching this and had I been given the option I would have escorted this older relative to his "great reward" personally. I was very surprised the boy had not tried to harm himself.

No one had been suspicious about this relative coming over because the person was "very religious" ...a church- goer. We have to be wise.

So now I knew exactly how to pray. I rebuked the demon that was controlling this older relative, and commanded him to leave the boy alone. I asked the Lord to remove this relative from the boy's life completely. And I also told the Lord that I know sometimes people who are victims of abuse, get marked somehow by the enemy so that they are abused all of their lives. I asked the Lord to set an angel with him permanently to keep this from happening. That was my prayer.

The Lord showed me a powerful angel had been assigned to protect the boy from any further abuse. This angel was about ten feet tall and looked very serious. I knew the boy would be safe. There would be no more abuse. I also found out that a week later, the abusive relative was permanently removed from his life. The Lord spoke to me about the situation and told me that now that the boy knew he was safe from harm, he could begin to heal. Thank you Jesus.

I can't go into any further details about this, but I wanted to show you why we must walk in the supernatural.

Prayer Trips

One of my favorite things to do is to go in the spirit to pray for people. Sometimes I pray for healing, sometimes for blessing or even deliverance. Here is my disclaimer... I do not set my own agenda in any way.

Many times people ask me to come and visit them in the spirit and pray for them or tell them things about themselves etc.. Very seldom does this ever happen for me. I can count the times on one hand and even then I rarely feel a need to mention what happened. I just see what God wants me to see and then pray how He wants me to pray. There is usually no need to talk about the event itself unless there is a purpose to do so.

But prayer trips in the unseen realm are awesome because among other reasons, I like to lay hands on people when I pray. If they live far away and it is not physically possible, it is possible in the spirit. Also in the spirit, doubt and unbelief do not seem to function like they do in the natural. In the spirit you are acutely aware of your authority. So there are many good reasons to go and pray in the spirit.

The Lord has allowed me to go to many different places across the globe to pray for people. Many of the prayer requests I receive are people to whom the Lord takes me to pray. I have prayed in the spirit for about every situation and malady that you can think of.

What does this look like? Let me explain....

I was praying for a young woman once and not seeing the results I felt she should be seeing. I felt led of the Lord to go to her home in the spirit and lay hands on her head and pray again.

I saw myself in my imagination flying to her house and walking in and laying hands on her and praying for her. As simple as that. I had to do this a couple of times before I knew that it was really happening. The third time, I walked into her home and saw her sitting on the couch with her head leaned back and her eyes closed. I simply walked up and laid my hands on her head and prayed.

Should you just barge into people's homes in the spirit? No, of course not. This is why we have to be led of the Lord in everything we do including supernatural translation or transportation.

The Lord Invited Me

One very cool thing happened not too long ago. I was praying and suddenly found myself sitting in a large conference room with about a dozen men and women. The meeting was a private meeting being held by the leader of a very well know ministry. I got to sit there with an angel and listen in for only a few minutes, for a specific reason. Then I came back home. It was a very rewarding few minutes though!

When You Don't Know How to Pray

About eight thousand miles away there lives a woman I have met a few times. This woman was having some very serious health issues. It was one of those things that causes pain and moves around so much that the doctors can't really narrow it down. I had prayed for her several times when I heard that she was really in serious pain and was losing hope.

The Lord led me to visit her in the spiritual realm and pray for her. It was early morning when I walked through her door. I mean I literally walked through it. She was asleep on her couch with her head propped up on one of the couch arms. I knelt by her head and laid my hand on her. I prayed for her for about ten minutes. I prayed mostly in tongues and I was really just relying on the Holy Spirit to use me as a vessel and do what He does.

I came back four times all together. Almost every time she was laying on the couch but once. That time she was seated at the dining room table. I prayed the same way I had previously and I believe that even though she may have sensed something, I don't think she had a clue as to the fact that the Lord had led me to pray for her. She obviously did not see me or sense my presence. But she did get better!

It was about a week or so later that I heard from her and there was no mention of pain or sickness or anything like that. Only normal conversion about regular life issues. I believe there are a couple things going on in this scenario. First, I believe there can be something powerful in the laying on of hands. We can impart something that we carry from God. Secondly, there is an increased faith in the spiritual dimension. Between the two, it was exactly what God wanted to see happen.

Wherever Your Foot Treads

I will give you every place where you set your foot, as I promised Moses. (Joshua 1;3)

I heard an awesome testimony once about Joshua Mills being translated to China and attending a prayer meeting there. If you get the chance you should search it out. It's a great testimony. He said he believes that he was taken there so that his foot would be upon Chinese soil. With his foot being upon Chinese soil he would have the legal right given in Joshua chapter one.

I try to do the same thing over the areas and people and places that I feel called to and love. On any given night, with the blessing of the Father, you can find me walking laps around the houses of my loved ones, in the spirit realm. I walk and declare and decree God's blessing and provision over them.

Be led of the spirit in everything you do. You don't want to do things just because it seems like a good idea. Remember that we only do those things that we see the Father do.

Most of the time, I just walk around the perimeter a few times and then either come back home or move on to the next place. Sometimes I feel compelled to go inside and pray and so I do that as well. Sometimes I am led to pray specifically for the needs of the people and/or loved ones I am visiting, so I do that too.

Many times new things that the Lord is teaching me I still have to take hold of by faith. The first time you ask the Lord to highlight someone that you can visit and pray over, it might feel totally pretend. It always does when you are learning about the spiritual realm. Don't let that throw you. Anything that you have learned that is worthwhile has been gained through a process of learning and increase. It is the same with spiritual things.

I was in a vision or experience once and I met and talked to Bob Jones the very well-known prophet. I don't know that it was actually him or an angel that looked like him or what, but he told me something that is very true. He said...

"Whenever you are somewhere in the spiritual realm and you see it and experience it with full awareness and clarity it means that you have been there many times."

I have found this to be the case. (Forgive me if I repeat myself but I really want you to get it and learn how to access the heavenly realms.) If you take one thing and engage, one trip, one access point, one step of faith and immerse yourself fully into it you will see the fruit of what I was told that day.

You will start out seeing it in your imagination by faith. That might happen the first ten or fifteen times and then something begins to shift and your awareness increases. This will continue until you come into the fullness of the realm you are engaging. If a person hopscotches around trying to find that experience it will elude them every time.

Pray From That Heavenly Place

If you are going to be praying anyway, I would advise you to pray in the spirit. Pray from that Heavenly place where you know who you are and your spirit is not being impeded by your flesh or soul. Go in the spirit and pray in the spirit.

9
ENCOUNTERING DARKNESS

There is a reality that we as believers are engaged in a battle. Whether a person has the ability to see the battle or not, we are still in it. The Bible clearly states the truth about these things and we have to understand from a biblical reality. It appears that too many Christians have an understanding about the spiritual realm and how it works that is gained from some Hollywood plot.

As I relay a few instances about encountering darkness in the spirit please know that we do not have to be in fear. The Bible tells us so many times "fear not!" We need to listen and understand. The Lord has empowered and equipped us for our work. The Lord has not given us a spirit of fear. But He has given us a lot of other things. If you don't know who you are in Christ, you need to learn anyway. Whether you are seeking the deep things of God or just sharing the love of

Christ with your family, you need to know who you are.

Many Christians have a false understanding about the spiritual realm which creates for them an atmosphere of fear. We are already in the spiritual realm. The thing that we are missing is understanding and awareness. Once we begin to be aware, we can learn. It is not that suddenly we have encountered it because we see it. We are in both realms every day, all day.

So if this part in any way causes you fear or worry, learn something about who you are. If you believe that you should not think about this part of the journey, again learn who you are.

Blazing New Trails

I found out a long time ago that evil spirits inhabit the spiritual realm. It's a no-brainer right? When you see or go into the spiritual dimension there is a chance that sometimes you will see such things. This is especially true if the Lord is leading you to help someone or deal with something from your place of authority.

Many say "I don't want to see that." I understand why. However if you can see what is tempting you it makes it easier to rebuke it and deal with it. If you can see the spirit afflicting the person you are praying for it makes it that much easier to deal with it. There is no upside to being spiritually blind even though so many think there is.

Many times the experiences I have are brand new. I mean that because this walk is new for me, I am very much learning as I go. So many of the things I experience are new things . I believe that for most of you this will be the same.

It's nice when the new experience is a new angel that you meet or a heavenly place you encounter but there is also the "other camp" and it's real.

Walk in wisdom, follow God's voice and be assured that it's all part of our mandate to be like Jesus and destroy the works of the devil. You will learn and adjust just fine.

Places of Captivity in the Spirit

I did not know a thing about this when I had my first real lesson about the places or regions of captivity.

The first experience I had with the regions of captivity was my own personal deliverance from some type of "coldness" that was affecting my emotions toward my wife and daughter. Here is a little back story...

For some time, perhaps a year or more, I had been feeling an emotional distance between me and my wife and daughter. I could think of no logical reason for this. I loved them both dearly and wanted to show them the affection that I felt. But there was a coldness of some sort that kept me from feeling that closeness.

One night in the middle of the night I awoke to find myself in a small enclosure like a prison cell with a barred door. I was wide awake with all my faculties and full conscious awareness and this was in no way just a bad dream. The iron bars of the cell door were on fire. As freaked out as I was by all this, the Lord had still given me the presence of mind to use the name of Jesus. I raised my hand and struck at the door *as if* I had a sword, two times. I shouted "fall in the name of Jesus" twice also.

The door fell and I walked out of the cell. There was a long narrow stairway just on the other side of the bars and I walked up the stairway and out of the darkness. At the top of the stairs there was a door. I opened the door and stepped through and into the light. On the other side of the door I saw my wife and daughter and they were both glowing beautifully. It was at that moment that I was completely restored in my relationship to them. I was delivered.

This was both a lesson for me and a forecast of things to come. I found that I would be seeing many such places in the years to come for various reasons.

So what happened? Was I transported to that awful place? And if I was taken there how did that help me? No I believe that as I laid in bed that night the Lord allowed me to be aware of a place I was already in in another dimension. Once I was aware, I knew that I needed to leave that place. And that's when I commanded the cell doors to fall and came out.

I had read about this in a book by Ana Mendez Ferrell called "Regions of Captivity" about a year later. She talks in the book about the very thing that I experienced. She said that many people can't receive or hold their deliverance because there is a part of them that is captured by the enemy where the enemy has influence over us in our soul. I would not even write about this if I had not learned it to be true. It is true.

One of the things that I have noticed for me anyway, was that very often when I pray for the Lord to sanctify me or purify me or move me to a place of greater Glory, one of several things begins to happen. All kinds of "junk" begins to be dredged up out of me or people start provoking me (such as when I asked the Lord to give me more patience) or I start finding myself in these places of captivity. I wish I could say it has only happened once or twice but it has happened many times.

My Deliverance from Cigarettes

Years ago I smoked and had prayed many times asking the Lord to deliver me from it. I had tried quitting dozens of times and it never really stuck. I would quit for a month or I would quit for an hour but I was fed up with trying. One day I prayed. "Lord, I'm done trying to quit. If you don't want me to smoke, you are going to have to take it from me."

Only a few days later as I drove home from work one Friday, I became so tired, I could hardly make it home. I stumbled up the sidewalk, fell into the house on the living room floor and slept until the next day.

When I awoke, I had no desire whatsoever for smoking. The Lord completely delivered me. However I still would have these dreams where I would be smoking. The dreams became fewer and fewer, but still I would have them. And even sometimes I would actually smell smoke as if I was standing in the middle of a smokers breakroom. This went on for a long time.

One night I woke up seated in a café of sorts. It was full of people. I don't think there was an empty seat. Everyone in the entire place was smoking except me. I was at a loss as to what to do. The smell was horrible. I never liked being in a smoker's breakroom even when I smoked because of the intensity of the smell. There were people in the place who were engaging me in conversation and acting like everything was as normal as could be. I got up and walked out of the place.

I believe that this tie that I had on me or this place that had influence on my soul was what had allowed the dreams and even the fact that I smelled smoke so clearly.

Tight Spaces

Once I woke up in a small box. There was not even hardly enough room to move. There were two beings that were standing outside of the box and I believe them to be evil spirits. The door was opened for me. I knew that I could come out if I chose to. But instead of coming out, I make a couple of stupid jokes about being in captivity.

The Lord used this to show me that my "humor" although many times it is fine, is sometimes something I use to give excuse to things, bondages and behaviors that I should not tolerate. I was shown to never joke about bondage in any way. If I did, it was a permission of sorts for the enemy to continue to keep me in bondage.

Wide Open Spaces

I had an issue at one time in my life with flying. No, I wasn't afraid to fly, I found out that in the spirit one can fly and I enjoyed it a bit too much.

I was in the spirit one day and I looked around me and saw beautiful wide open spaces as far as the eye could see. It looked like the clouds went on forever and my first thought was to fly. I did fly for a while and it was exciting but when I flew very high I suddenly hit a ceiling of sorts. What looked like open sky was a fake sky. I examined the place more fully and soon found that when I tested all the boundaries, I was completely enclosed in a place that only *appeared* to be open and unobstructed. Once I realized that I was locked in, it didn't feels so good anymore. I tried to bust through the false ceiling and get out but was not able to do so. I believe that when an angel showed up one day to talk to me about this subject, I was released from that bondage.

Dark Places

Many of these places of spiritual influence have been very dark. I almost always realize that I can bring light into these encounters. Many times there are others around who don't like the light and curse when the place is illuminated.

The common theme in all of these regions of captivity is that you are really captive. Either by walls or fire or darkness, I would feel very hemmed in. Some of these places were deep pits that you could not climb out of. Other places were like dark hallways where there were angry and miserable souls. Many times there would be rooms and corridors that were very bleak as well as dark.

There would also be a couple different kinds of beings in these places. There were sometimes demonic beings who were guarding these places and sometimes there would be the souls of people. Some of the people would be believers and some were unbelievers. The common theme among these beings and people or souls was anger and hatred, a love of darkness and a hatred of me because I knew that I did not belong and would always call for God's light.

The Purpose of Seeing these Places

I believe that the Lord allows us (me) to see these places so that we can know the areas where we still need deliverance and/or sanctification. Does this mean that we are walking in sin or are in manifested bondage? No, it does not. I asked the Lord about this one day and He gave me the answer and the confirmation.

The Lord told me that many times we have the influence of the enemy around our lives even though we have been born again. This is especially true for those who are newly saved or who are not fully grounded. The Lord explained that as a person matures and yields to the Spirit, the chains and influence of the enemy are removed.

So we can be delivered from anger let's say, and we can walk in peace and be full of the joy of the Lord. But full deliverance with the removal of the legal chains upon us may happen a little later once we can hold our ground so to speak. The Lord talked to me about the fact that if a person is completely delivered but is still partly drawn to sin, the enemy can come back bringing even more wicked spirits.

Then it goes and takes with it seven other spirits more wicked than itself, and they go in and live there. And the final condition of that person is worse than the first. That is how it will be with this wicked generation." (Matthew 12:45)

However if we see that we are still being influenced by actually seeing these places, It helps us know how to pray.

Can We Be Deceived?

The answer is yes. There is always the possibility of that. That is why we need to walk circumspectly and not as fools. We need to stay close to the Lord and not get full of ourselves. We need to daily acknowledge our need and dependence upon the Holy Spirit.

We also have to practice putting beings to the question. Meaning *"Has Jesus Christ come in the flesh?"* Maybe you think that you might offend an angel or a saint or the Lord if you do this but we have to remember that He gave us this test for a good reason. Many people have fallen into deception because they don't test the spirits. Test them. No one will get offended except those who are of the enemy.

Last year I posed this question to an evil spirit who was trying to appear as being from God. I put the question to him and he got angry. He said *"Why do you people always have to ask that?!"*

Being in the spirit or going in the spirit opens the possibility for more direct confrontation. The evil spirits don't like this because it is easier for them to deceive you if you don't realize that they are there. If you see them openly they have to try harder to lure you rather than just speak to your mind as they do most of the time.

What do these "confrontations" normally look like? Many people have a "Hollywood" conception of what it looks like. (as I have already mentioned) The reality is that most of the confrontations that I have had have been along the lines of evil spirits trying to lure me or seduce me back into some kind of sin. They try to woo and seduce with their lies and get you to agree with them.

If they were to attack us outright, first of all we can call on the Lord and we might do so out of fear. They don't want that to happen. They don't want to provoke us into battle.

They would much rather keep us off guard and then trick us into falling back into old sins or temptations. Most evil spirits do not want to tip their hand and lose whatever control or access that they may have.

Other Beings

I have seen souls in various states and it is a little difficult to understand always what we are seeing or encountering without a word from God. Sometimes things fly by you so quick that you don't have time to say anything let alone ask them a question.

I have also found that this is all very much a learning process. We don't have to be in fear but be aware that He has given His angels charge over us. I learned this one night when I transitioned from my prayer chair to the spiritual realm.

On this occasion I had been praying in my prayer chair and fell asleep. I then found myself waking from sleep in the spirit realm. As I looked in the spirit I saw what I thought was a tormented human soul. He held out his hand to me and said *"Hurry! take my hand, I'm going to Hades!"*.

I took his hand and immediately felt as if I was moving somewhere in the spirit, so I quickly let go. He again said it even more insistently *"Hurry! Take my hand, I'm going to Hades!"*. So I again took his hand and immediately found myself moving somewhere again. This time however someone intervened and rebuked me gently like you might rebuke a child who doesn't know better. (Most likely an angel) He said *"Where do you think you're going?!"* And I again let go with the knowledge that I should not do that again.

I honestly believe that I thought I was going to help someone from going to Hades by taking their hand.

We have to be aware in the spirit and realize that there are deceiving spirits who will try to lead us the wrong way if they can. That's why the Bible says...

Dear friends, do not believe every spirit, but test the spirits to see whether they are from God, because many false prophets have gone out into the world. This is how you can recognize the spirit of God: Every spirit that acknowledges that Jesus Christ has come in the flesh is from God.(1 John 4:1-2)

One night I also saw a being that looked very much like a dragon that you might see in the movies. The funny thing was I knew that he was protecting me. The look in his eyes was something I won't forget. As crazy as it might sound I believe it was a seraphim. He was huge. I know that the Lord has set an incredible amount of protection around us. (meaning you and I) I have seen various warriors, shields, chain mail, swords and angels physically acting as a covering over us as we slept.

I'll Be Back

There are a couple of places that I believe have been given to me. Just as there are for you. My home, family and property is one of them. Another place is in a different country and it is a place I have been to in the spirit a few times. One night as I was praying, I started thinking about this place.

Suddenly I began moving and flying and pretty soon I was flying over the country and coming down into a certain street. It was very strange how I "landed". I flew into the mouth of the street and then touched down kind of the way you see superman do it in the movies. Then I began walking.

At a table in the distance I saw three witches who were also in the spirit and were not visible to those around them. I knew that they enjoyed this power. I walked directly over to their table and said "hello". They all stared at me.

"You can see us?" one of them asked me. I said "Of course I can see you." Immediately I knew they were all questioning in their minds who I was and why I could see them. As I saw these thoughts spinning around, I felt led of the Lord to say *"I have to go now... but I'll be back."* And I walked away.

In speaking about these dark things, I am doing so because I really want you to be prepared. There are so many people who already experience these types of things that to be informed is not a bad thing. It is a part of our calling...to destroy the works of the devil.

We only have to be aware of who we really are and we will walk in authority and dominion over the enemy.

We are sons of God, formed in His likeness, seated in heavenly places in Christ. We are legal heirs to the Kingdom of Heaven, joint heirs with Christ. We are seated in authority far above principalities and powers. We are one spirit with God. As He is, so are we in this world.

Just so there is no confusion... this is why we should be bold.

MICHAEL VAN VLYMEN

10

THE HEAVENLY REALMS

In my thirtieth year, in the fourth month on the fifth day, while I was among the exiles by the Kebar River, the heavens were opened and I saw visions of God. (Ezekiel 1:1)

In the book of Revelation, John talks about hearing a voice telling him to "come up here."

After this I looked, and there before me was a door standing open in heaven. And the voice I had first heard speaking to me like a trumpet said, "Come up here, and I will show you what must take place after this." (Revelation 4:1)

The Lord is still telling us to "come up here." I remember in the book of Matthew the Lord rebuked the Pharisees because they didn't want to enter the heavenly realms and prevented others from doing so as well. Even in that day there were those religious leaders who were offended with people wanting to have and having that close relationship with God.

Woe to you, teachers of the law and Pharisees, you hypocrites! You shut the door of the kingdom of heaven in people's faces. You yourselves do not enter, nor will you let those enter who are trying to. (Matthew 23:13)

My very first experience in the heavenly realm was with the Lord Jesus, who took me to a high place in the stars and spoke to me. Although I have not had as many experiences in Heavens as I have had across the Earth, I have had several experiences in the heavenly places with angels and saints.

Many of my journeys into heavenly places have also started out in my prayer chair. That place of prayer really has turned out to be a great place to be, to be positioned for the supernatural things of God. One of my very first journeys was cut short due to demonic interference.

The Park

I had entered into a heavenly park one night in the spirit and was completely overwhelmed by the beauty of the place. The lawns were so beautiful and green. Rolling hills and colorful flowers were all around. Everything about the place was beautiful and alive! I was excited to have the chance to see it. All at once I felt someone slip a bag of some sort over my head and then I could see nothing. I did not know what to do at the time and ended up back at home in the natural realm.

Any time something happens like this or if anything happens that confuses you or startles you or even if something is trying to pull you out of the spiritual realm, just relax and look for and expect God to do something to help you. Do not allow it to throw you. If you get worked up, it will only hasten your return to the natural realm.

The Stars

This journey has been one that has happened fairly often. It doesn't seem to take much to propel you into the stars. Maybe because it's such an exciting proposition or maybe the Lord wants us to be amazed by His creation and enjoy it close up. Either way it is an awesome thing.

Early on in my foray into the clouds and the stars, I was rebuked by an angel for seeking the supernatural apart from God. It made me wary to only do the right thing. To only seek those experiences and journeys in the spiritual realms that were sanctioned by the Lord. It wasn't long after the rebuke (a couple weeks) that another angel showed up and ended up taking me flying with him. So I gained an understanding that it was fine to travel supernaturally as long as it was as a son and not as a random thrill seeker.

One of my earlier trips was a journey that went from prayer, to sleep, to wide awake and rocketing through the stars. I was traveling so fast I could not myself believe it. With full awareness of the stars and nebulas and space, awareness of the cold and the feeling of it on my spiritual body, I had no plans of stopping. I just went. At some point I was aware that someone or something stopped me and brought me back. More than likely an angel that figured I had had enough.

One night I was praying in my prayer chair and I decided that I would go into the spirit and do a prayer walk around the property. As I have already told you, I knew that if I engaged my imagination in an outrageous way, the connection to the spiritual realm would happen much faster. So I saw myself going through the ceiling to the roof.

It only took minutes to be fully engaged in the spiritual dimension, walking on my roof and praying and worshipping. Did you know that you can yell and sing really loudly in the spirit? That's what I did. I was jumping up and spinning in the spirit on the roof and yelling and singing

"Jesus is Lord!" and "Jesus is King!" and all sorts of other declarations about the Lord.

After ten or twenty minutes of this I was launched into the stars. I flew into the stars and enjoyed worshipping from that heavenly place and not too long after that I came back.

Rings of Transportation

I once heard Brother Sadhu Sundar Selvaraj talk about being transported in the spiritual dimension in rings of energy of some sort. Much like in the movies, these rings would come down over someone and lift them and transport them. It reminds me of Ezekiel's wheels.

One night I laid down to sleep and was calling on the Lord as I fell asleep. Suddenly I began to realize that I was in the spirit realm. In the past if I thought I might be in the spirit, I would fly. If I wasn't able to fly, then I would know that I was just awake in the natural realm. (world) But due to my rebuke from the angel, this was not an option to me.

I somehow found myself in a dark and dusty corridor of some sort, where all of the connecting corridors were also dark and dusty. It was not the type of place I like to be when I am in the spirit. At times I have "explored" these types of corridors and dark places, but I do not like such places. The only things I meet in those types of places are unclean spirits and demonic beings. As I pondered what to do, I remembered what I heard someone say once about moving in the spirit realm. It was said that in the spirit, always go up to heavenly places. Don't go to and fro because it's too easy to bring back "critters" that will try to mess up your life. So I found a way to climb up higher and when I got so high, I began to fly up into the heavenly realms. By faith.

As I flew higher and higher, I flew past stars and clusters of stars. Then I found myself even above the stars and still flying higher. As I flew, I looked toward where I was flying to and saw many, many spiritual beings up ahead in the distance. As I approached them I thought that they might be demonic beings trying to stop me or attack me. I was fearful for just a few seconds.

The closer I got to them, I realized that these beings were indeed angels and they had arranged themselves in rings of sorts, kind of like angelic portals to travel through. There were several rings of angels that I went through, and as I got close to the top ring of angels I actually began to move right into the path of one of the angels in the ring. Once again I felt a bit of fear from this. As I braced myself for impact, I extended my arms and spread out my open palms toward him to soften the blow. But when I reached the angel, he slapped my open palms with his, kind of like giving me a high five! When he did this it propelled me even higher into the Heavens!

The Lord sets His angels around us to help us and watch over us! They are always around, always on the job. What an incredible experience that was.

Meeting Storm Clouds

One night I began moving in the spirit and found myself traveling across plains and fields of grain and then came to a pass of some sort between two mountains. I was standing in the fields not far from the mountains, the wind was really blowing and I could feel it and it felt good. The sensations in the spiritual realm (at least the nice ones) are incredible.

I felt that I should go closer to the pass and I went up the side of the mountain and was standing in a semi secluded place where I could observe whatever was going on. I did not have a sense of what I was about to see so it came as a complete surprise. I was watching the sky through the pass and I saw giant storm clouds approaching the pass. They began to come through the pass, almost as if they were being born or formed there. They were huge and I was in awe.

As I examined the storm clouds I suddenly realized that they all had faces and expressions on their faces. I saw that each storm cloud had it's own personality and I moved closer to have a better look. As I was then standing there more or less exposed, I was watching and examining each cloud pass by with astonishment on my face. As the fourth or fifth cloud passed by me I was staring at him hard just totally taken by what I was seeing and experiencing. Suddenly the cloud turned his face toward me and looked at me hard and quickly drew close to me for just a moment before he then moved away with all of the others. It startled me a little as I had never seen anything like this before. Ok... It scared me but only momentarily.

The Courtrooms of Heaven

This is one place that I have been hearing a lot about lately. I did not know of it from the perspective that so many others have. I have been asked if I have been in the courtrooms of Heaven and as far as I knew, I had only had awareness of being there twice with only limited vision of what the place looked like and what was going on. I stood back away from everything but still felt like I was intruding somehow in what was happening there.

After having been asked many times by people about the courtrooms of Heaven I decided to check out the teaching by Robert Henderson to see if they might launch me into further revelation about them. What I found pleased me as I soon learned that the protocol of being in the heavenly courtroom and the way Brother Robert teaches people to engage was something that I have been doing for many years by faith! So it gave me an awareness that I could also go deeper into this experience in the courtrooms and I am expecting to.

I believe that the Lord wants us to be mature and learn about spiritual realities such as the courts. He honors what we do in faith but we can also know much more about them too.

Meeting the Lord in Heavenly Places

Many times the things that I experience are born out of the testimonies of others. I had heard some awesome testimonies from Bruce Allen and Kevin Basconi, Bob Jones and others. I am always telling the Lord "We want that!" We as in my family. It doesn't cost anything extra to include others in our prayers. And if I know friends and other people who are seeking the deep things also, I throw them in as well.

But these testimonies of spending time with the Lord Jesus have been the ones that really capture my attention. There is a part of me that says we can almost expect angels to show up around our lives but a visit from the Lord.... Wow! That is something! I know we should be looking for face to face encounters with Jesus. But I think many of you can relate to my thinking on this one.

I heard about a place In Heaven from the testimony of someone who had been there. He described the place fairly well and I thought that I would like to try and find it. I had an image in my mind to start with and I just began to engage that image in prayer, desiring to be with the Lord Jesus.

It took me a little time before I entered into the reality of the building I was searching for and explored the building just a little. If there are others of you who have been to this building in Heaven you may recognize it from my description.

The first few times that I saw this building it was very vague. I saw it more clearly the more I went there and learned more about it. As you walked to this building the first thing you might notice is the size. It is a massive but beautiful three or four story structure that looks very much like a castle of sorts. The walls look like smooth limestone all fitted together perfectly. The building itself is on a rolling hill and the main entrance is on the high side of the hill. There is a stone walkway that leads to the front entrance.

Also, before you would get to the main entrance there is a walkway that splits off and goes down to the lower side of the building. It curves gently around the building and there are gardens and flowers along that walkway. There are also benched along that path. I explored that lower path twice just to see what was there.

I walked the main walkway to the entrance, and entered directly into a hallway. This hall was very tall. If I had to guess I would say twenty feet or more, and there were rooms or doors along both sides of the hallway. I also noticed portraits on the walls in the hallway but I don't recall who they were.

The rooms that I always went to were about half way down this main hall and on the left side. One room was small and looked like a changing room to get ready. And that did happen to me a couple of times. I was made ready. The other room that I went to was quite large and was more like a banquet hall. I went to that place several times and met with the Lord there. Sometimes I would be brought in and He would already be there and other times I would have to wait for a little while.

There was a table not too far from the entrance to the room and sometimes we sat at the table. Many times I asked to sit at His feet and He allowed it but would always bring me up to sit with Him also. The things that we talked about were just personal things having to do with life. I always loved spending this time with Him and He never rushed me.

Engaging the things of Heaven is something I would encourage you to do. Start out by faith in your imagination and allow the Lord to bring you up. We are living in a special time and if you will do this it will bear much fruit.

There is one other place that I go to in Heaven and that is the Throne Room. I actually went to the Throne Room before I went to the hall I just described.

The Throne Room

I started seeing the Throne Room rather vaguely at first. I knew I wanted to worship the Lord in the heavenly realm and I began by faith but for some reason it opened up rather quickly. The first few times that I went I would try to almost hide way in the back behind people (or angels) and always within seconds the Lord would cause me to be moved to the front row, real close to Him.

After I stopped trying to keep my distance I was able to be a part and stand in other places but still He brings me closer sometimes.

I usually find myself on my knees , sometimes prone and even standing a few times. I have been able to see more the more I go and I will try to describe what I see there.

The Throne is huge. It's hard for me to tell how huge but it fills the sky. The front appear to me to be curved and there are lampstands along the front. The colors are white and gold of varying hues and light. I'm sure there are other colors as well but those are the ones that stand out to me. I believe the atmosphere around the throne is multi-colored though.

I feel like I am in a huge amphitheater when I am there. The atmosphere is continuous worship yet even though the place is filled with countless others there is a feeling of personal connection to the Lord in that place. Kind of like the same way He brought me to the front, that personal connection is always there.

As I write this I am reminded that I should most definitely be spending more time in this place with the Lord.

One thing I ask from the LORD, this only do I seek: that I may dwell in the house of the LORD all the days of my life, to gaze on the beauty of the LORD and to seek him in his temple. (Psalm 27:4)

Heavenly Mansions and the Abodes of Angels

The first time I saw heavenly mansions I was amazed at the size. I don't know if they are all that size. But I did see some mansions that had forty or fifty foot columns in front. The streets were very wide and the areas around the mansions were very spacious. The ones I saw were all stone.

I also saw the one I believe is mine. It has a courtyard and off the courtyard a wide stairway that leads up to a kind of large second story patio type area that then leads into a large room with no doors on it. There were only light curtains draped across the entrance.

It is a beautiful place, exactly the kind of place I would love which is way I believe it might be mine. Plus the fact that it felt like home.

I have been to at least two places that I believe are the estates of angels. One was vast and sprawling and had many, many houses on it and I believe that may have had something to do with his position and authority. The other one was also quite large but it had a different feel for lack of a better word. Both of the angels were very nice. One of them had a much more serious demeanor and talked to me about some very specific things. The other one showed me some answers to things that I had questions about.

Heavenly Provision

I have heard several of my friends and others talk about different places in Heaven. Places like the body parts room and the Library, the treasury and the Hall of Faith. I have not seen very much in Heaven. Most of my travel in the Spirit has been to other places, but I have seen some very interesting things.

On at least three occasions I have seen huge areas or buildings where angels get things that they need to help those of us on the Earth. The size of the buildings are massive. They remind me of hangers for aircraft only much, much bigger. The buildings had every type of thing you could ask for. I wandered around looking at everything for quite a while and no one seemed to mind a bit.

I saw angels standing in lines once, holding slips of paper and I had thought that perhaps they were getting assignments. Now in hindsight, I think the papers might have been requisition for the things they were getting there as their supplies.

We can ask for things we need and the Lord has provision ready for us. Sometimes it seems as if we don't know whether the things we need will ever get to us. There is a principle that I like very much. It is found in the following scripture.

So I say to you: Ask and it will be given to you; seek and you will find; knock and the door will be opened to you. (Luke 11:9)

Another translation says...

So I say to you: Keep asking, and it will be given you. Keep searching, and you will find. Keep knocking, and the door will be opened for you. (Luke 11:9)

This second translation reminds me of the teaching concerning the unjust judge. If we refuse to grow weary and keep declaring or asking God's will to be manifested it will come to pass. I know many will read that and say "What if it's not God's will?" God can make it very clear if something is not His will. We don't have to be in confusion about this. I consider that every promise in the Word of God is available to me. I pray with the expectation that it does. If for some reason the Lord does not want me to have something He will tell me. Otherwise I keep pressing in and on.

Angels are ministering spirits sent on our behalf.

Once a few years ago, one of the angels who takes me places took me to a logistics center where angels were working and where provision was being made for the saints. It looked like a very serious and productive place.

Recently near the end of my stay in Germany, the airline Lufthansa went on strike. I needed to take a Lufthansa flight to catch my connecting flight to Chicago and I was thinking and praying about it. I got on my phone trying to get a hold of someone at Lufthansa to see what arrangements could be made and I wasn't having much success so I tried to contact American Airlines. I didn't want to wait on hold again because my minutes were costing a small fortune. I was feeling just a bit frustrated.

I received a series of messages from my friend Thomas who was taking care of all my arrangements while I was in Germany and he said he would help me to do whatever I decided to do. I felt better because I was confident that he could help me, but I really wanted to just make all my original connections and go home. I was a little "home sick".

With only a couple days until the original departure would have taken place, Once again I was thinking about this and praying about it. It was early in the morning as I was praying.

Suddenly the fact that this was an airline related problem reminded me of the place that I had been to in the spiritual realm that looked kind of like an airline terminal. I remembered once again seeing powerful angels there. A logistics center for the work of the angels. I decided that I would try to go back there if I could and see if they could help me.

In my imagination I focused on the place and how it looked and felt and I thought about being there. Suddenly I found that I was back there again. I had gone into the spiritual realm and to this place just by imagining it.

I still wasn't sure exactly what I should do when I got there because the only other time that I had been there, an angel had taken me. So I entered the place and sat down on a bench by the door. Within a minute and angel came over to me. I began to explain to him about Lufthansa and the strike and ask him for help with my situation when he stopped me and said "You don't need to worry. Everything is all taken care of." Then he turned and walked away and went back to what he had been doing.

I went back to the hotel (the natural realm) and I was able to relax and have peace that the Lord had taken care of it for me. When I finally made it to the airport the day of my departure, Lufthansa was still on strike but my flight was still operating. I made all my original flights and connections and even arrived a little early back home.

Going into the heavenly realms is a provision God has given us to get the things we need. Whether it is wisdom or understanding, financial blessings or any other need the Lord has provision in the Kingdom for us. Go into the heavens and the Kingdom. It is yours. It is your inheritance.

11
MOVING THROUGH TIME

I absolutely believe that God can do anything. I believe that He can even do things that are way beyond my ability to understand. That's o.k. The ability to move through time is one of those peculiar things that many people make a problem with. The Bible talks about the fact that God has and does alter time.

So the sun stood still, and the moon stopped, till the nation avenged itself on its enemies, as it is written in the Book of Jashar. The sun stopped in the middle of the sky and delayed going down about a full day. (Joshua 10:13)

We see from this scripture that the Lord held time still for a full day. This seems very strange to some of us only because we have allowed the world and it's wisdom and systems to set the parameters of what is possible and what is not. Even in regards to the understanding of the Bible and more specifically God's power, we allow natural understanding to set the boundaries in most cases.

In theory at least, we understand that time exists in God. He created everything that we measure the movement of time by. As knowledge increases and science catches up with the Bible, we see through quantum mechanics that movement through time is completely possible. The jury seems to still be out for many, but even those who say that tie travel is not functionally possible say that it is theoretically possible.

Either way, once you have experienced something it makes it nearly impossible to believe against that experience no matter how "compelling" the argument. There are many people across the face of the Earth who don't have the luxury or unbelief. It's too late.

A Tent Meeting in Time

One of the two earliest experiences that I have had with this phenomenon was the attendance of a tent revival type meeting that I would say had the appearance of the nineteen-fifties.

My prayer chair was my starting point that day and I was not seeking to move through time or go anywhere, but was waiting on the Lord to show me something. I did not have a very clear vision in this situation however. I saw a big tent with a dividing wall of canvas and being in the spirit, I had a strong spiritual perception that half of the people there were hungry for God and the other half were just attending.

Much like many of the churches today, I saw it was the same then. The hungry were receiving from God and the others were oblivious to His presence.

A Healing Crusade

My second experience moving through time was the time I was translated to a healing meeting in a huge theater of some sort. I don't know where the meeting was that was taking place. There was about a fifteen foot space between the stage and the first row and I was seated to the right on the first row. I remember that the people were also dressed in the same manner that those from the voice of healing era were dressed in.

The person speaking was not someone that I recognized. It was not Brother Branham or Paul Cain or Jack Coe but that doesn't necessarily mean that they were not well known, just that I had never seen them.

I was there for at least forty-five minutes and had great awareness in the experience. However I did not retain conscious knowledge of the message when I returned.

Turn Back the Clock Lord

During this past year I have been stretching the boundaries with my steps of faith to encounter the Kingdom. It is not uncommon for me to lay hands on my vehicle and decree that my upcoming trip should also include me traveling through time in some way, or instantly arriving at my destination. (which is kind of the same thing)

On this particular day I did neither. I was running late for work and I was just a bit upset about it. I realized that if I left right away I could almost make it in time. However, when I jumped in my van I saw that my tank was on empty. I resigned myself to the fact that I would be late.

I left the house at six forty-five and headed to the gas station. When I arrived at the gas station I checked my watch again to see how I was doing and the time now said six twenty-two. I moved back twenty or more minutes in time.

The really funny thing about this was that I was still three minutes late! I learned something about believing for things like this though.

Taking Back the Land

This last example is one of my favorite experiences. I spent the early part of the night in my prayer chair and went to bed around two a.m. Not long after laying down, I woke up. I woke up sitting on a horse. I was wearing some kind of armor and carrying a sword. The horse and I were crossing what looked like a huge battle field and there were weapons scattered all over and several spears that had banners were stuck into the ground.

There was what appeared to be a small village in the close distance and at the edge of the town were three men standing between the town and the battlefield. As I got close to the men they walked toward me as if to stop me and I held out the sword toward them and just looked at them and they backed away. From the appearance of the town, the weapons and the men, I would guess we were in the fifteen hundreds.

As I rode into the town I could see mainly women and children. They looked fearful and wary of me. Then there was a woman that saw me and started to run. She ran through the streets going through buildings and alleys and I followed her by the spirit. She would up hiding in some kind of mill of some sort. And I knew she was inside but the Lord told me it was time to go. Just before I was transported back, the Lord gave me the understanding of what was going on. There was a witch who rose up to take advantage of all the people who were left after the battle that had happened. She had the entire town in fear. When all the people saw her running through the streets terrified and trying to hide from me, the fear of her was broken. Then the Lord translated me back home.

Confirming Testimonies

One thing that I am very happy about is that God confirms what He does. I have heard many testimonies of others going back into time to attend meetings and crusades and other events. Many of those people remember all the details of the translation.

Many others from well-known ministers to "regular" people have been transported back into time, sometimes centuries away to lead people to Christ or heal the sick or accomplish other things for the Kingdom.

Many believers are very challenged by these experiences. Many others are saying *"whatever you want to do God I'm willing."*

I don't know how this works. I just know that I cannot limit God to my natural intellect. That would be foolish. I'm still engaging these things by faith and hope you will too.

12

AN OPEN DOOR

Why Lord?

As the world gets darker and darker, it becomes clearer and clearer that we are here in this specific time for a reason.

For if you remain silent at this time, relief and deliverance for the Jews will arise from another place, but you and your father's family will perish. And who knows but that you have come to your royal position for such a time as this? (Esther 4:14)

See, darkness covers the earth and thick darkness is over the peoples, but the LORD rises upon you and his glory appears over you. (Isaiah 60:2)

The Bible talks about these times and also tells us about a

group of believers, special people sold out to God. I believe that the Word is talking about you and I.

As I talk to people about this subject and moving in the supernatural in general, I find that although there are several of us, the percentage of believing believers is very small.

It's estimated there are over two billion Christians in the world at the time of this writing. Few believe like the early church.

This is one reason I get so excited for all those who are seeking to walk in the supernatural. All you who desire to see and work with angels and move supernaturally and heal the sick and exercise authority over evil spirits and manifest miracles will be used. The Lord is raising you up. He is putting a fire in you, a discontent with the status quo. There may be a hundred thousand Christians in your town, but there are only six of you willing to pay the price and walk in miracles.

What I'm saying is that God uses the willing. If you are willing He will use you! He is no respecter of persons.

Arise, shine, for your light has come, and the glory of the LORD rises upon you. (Isaiah 60:1)

Why is This Necessary?

According to the Word, there is coming a time and even now is where movement for Christians and Christians functioning in everyday society will be greatly diminished.

"This know also, that in the LAST DAYS perilous times shall come..." (2 Timothy 3:1)

"Now the Spirit speaketh expressly, that in the latter times some shall depart from the faith, giving heed to seducing spirits, and doctrines of devils; Speaking lies in hypocrisy;

having their conscience seared with a hot iron." (1 Timothy 4:1-2)

Now there are many people who read a verse like this and unfortunately they think of those of us who heal the sick and cast out devils and believe in the supernatural things of God. I would say this is more a picture of modern day church.

...so that they could not buy or sell unless they had the mark, which is the name of the beast or the number of its name. (Revelation 13:17)

Although we might still be a few days from this happening, all the signs are there. Right now all over the world the movements of Christians are restricted. For those of us who still live in "free" countries, we are restricted as well. The Christian "rights" are being restricted at every turn and there is something new and wicked in the news every day it seems that tell us darkness has taken a stand against us. We know that. Now is the time for our light to shine.

In the coming days we can expect to see restrictions on travel, closed borders, restrictions on travel for Christians, an for ministry purposes. There will be countries that will be closed to us and provisions will be withheld from us.

Does that sound like gloom and doom? Well... in a way it is. It's not going to be pleasant. Just ask your brothers and sisters in the middle east right now. But the promise! That's what we have to be aware of! Isaiah sixty!

Those who are willing to shine will shine brighter than the noonday sun. This is not a metaphor. For those carrying God's glory , it will be seen on them!

Great Times of Miracles, Signs and Wonders

Those of you who say "yes Lord" will be used in ways that challenge you. Right now there are believers who are translating all over the world to preach the Gospel, to rescue people in harm's way, to heal and restore and raise the dead. There is no point in sugar coating any of this. You are going to do things that make people fear and tremble. The presence of God will so move through you that the wicked will be fearful to speak against you to your face. Those who serve the enemy will not want to challenge you.

I heard a testimony years ago from Dr. Lester Sumrall, one of my heroes. He said that as he was speaking with a witchdoctor in South America, the man told him that all the evil spirits that were normally around to do his bidding had left from fear. He told Dr. Sumrall that the brilliant light that surrounded him was like looking into the sun. That is the kind of thing we are talking about.

My own wife Gordana when the spirit of the Lord is upon her has visible electrical currents that come from her hands. It is clearly visible in the spirit realm. When those things begin to manifest in the natural, your testimony will carry weight that you never dreamed of. I have seen people clothed in light and clothed in fire. People have changed appearance in the Glory and it isn't something vague but discernable. Many people ministering across the world today take on the appearance of light as they speak. It is phenomenal! It's a testimony to God's power!

There are many reasons why God will use you and I in these ways in the days to come. Now is the time to lay hold of these truths and begin to practice. Practice the things of God. Exercise your senses! This is what God is doing.

Let Me Encourage You

Give yourself to the process. Learn to walk in both realms. There is a price to walk in these things but there is a higher price to not walk in them. Think about that. As we look around be aware that this is a special time. Please let these testimonies that I have shared with you be a springboard to launch you into greater things in God.

For I know the plans I have for you," declares the Lord, "plans to prosper you and not to harm you, plans to give you hope and a future. (Jeremiah 29:11)

God has set before you an open door. The Lord has given us the opportunity to be a part, to do something powerful and significant.... Something only we can do. That's the plan. We have a free will and we can choose His will. It's our choice. It wasn't that long ago I woke up several times in a row saying the words "Revelation three eight" over and over. When I looked it up I got the revelation. God has set before us an open door.

Thoughts and Feelings about the Spiritual Realm

The spiritual realm is an awesome place. The feelings of being in that realm are hard to describe. Every time I get asked to describe what it feels like to be in that realm, I say it's reality times ten. It is alive, it is like you feel you are alive. When I travel into the spiritual realm, I normally have full conscious awareness of being and going just as if I was in the natural realm but without my body. Of course the sensations are far above what we experience in the natural realm.

The transition from natural to spiritual is something that I believe people need to be aware of. The feeling of how and what your spirit feels like and the transition when your spirit takes the preeminent position. We get small tastes of it in great worship services but although we love and enjoy that feeling, we get used to the idea that it fades. We accept that.

Once you experience this you don't ever want to go back to "normal." I once had the opportunity to ask Gary Oates how to live in this place of continuous experience of the spiritual realm and he said "Your relationship with Christ. It all flows from that." That is absolutely true and everyone I know who has a powerful walk with God says the same thing.

We don't get enamored with the "stuff.' We get enamored with God and the stuff flows. The more you press into Him, the greater His kingdom manifests in your life. The more you worship Him, engage Him in prayer, look at Him and visit Him you will experience the fullness of life in Him.

Conversations with Jesus

As I have been following hard after God I have seen some incredible manifestations in the lives of others and I have asked the Lord about them. Once I asked the Lord about Joshua Mills. I said "Lord, why does he get all that awesome manifestation of your presence upon him and I don't. The Lord answered me immediately. He said "Why don't you try singing to me for two hours and see what happens." The Lord was just giving me a key. I was not condemned by that answer but I was enlightened by it.

I have heard other people say the same types of things about desiring the things that others walk in. We just have to know and believe that God is no respecter of persons. He withholds no good thing. Everything that I experience and more is for you. God will give you everything that you will passionately pursue.

I am learning that every time I hear a message or a word from someone who walks in something powerful, I pay attention to all the subtleties of what they say. Is God giving keys somehow hidden in little stories and encounters that they share? The answer is yes. God is speaking to us.

Step Through

This book is just a small piece of my life that I am sharing with you. It is in itself a doorway of sorts. I want you to know that everything is available for you and it is so phenomenal that we really don't even know what to ask for. Just step through by faith and let God direct your steps.

Our Family and the Spirit

Over the past several years the Lord has taken my family on a journey that still makes me want to pinch myself. All of us have seen the unseen realms and God has made Himself undeniably real to all of us.

Our testimonies of supernatural things in our lives is represented in all the books I write. That is really the purpose of everything I write, to show what God can and will do for you.

There are many, many more stories of translation and supernatural transportation in some of the other testimonies that I have shared in other writings. And the great thing is that this is far from over. Every day the Lord gives us new experiences and new testimonies. I have been asked before why I only seem to write about the supernatural of the Bible and the Kingdom. I do it because it is my little part that the Lord has given me. I am compelled to do my best to inform and equip people to walk in the supernatural.

Supernatural Friends

It seems that once you begin to walk in these types of things, the Lord gives you friends to fellowship with that walk in the same things. I have come to realize that He does this for a good reason. It's easy to succumb to the doubts and unbelief of those who have never experienced these things and who don't believe if that is your only fellowship. Having fellowship with others who experience the supernatural builds us up and encourages us. Whereas in many settings you may be the one who is "out there", among your supernatural friends you may actually be the tame one!

There really is nothing like this life in God where we really believe Him and do what He tells us to do. You have not tasted life until you have tasted Him. The Word says "Taste and see that the Lord is good!" He really is!

MICHAEL VAN VLYMEN

118

If you have never made the commitment to Jesus Christ I encourage you to do so now. Just pray this prayer and believe on Jesus.

A Prayer of Salvation

Dear Jesus,
I believe that you died on the cross to pay the penalty for my sins. I ask forgiveness for my sin and I turn to you as my Savior. Please come into my heart, fill me with your spirit and help me to live for you as you intended for me.

Amen

A Prayer of Consecration

Father, as we seek to know you more, let the blood of Jesus cover us and protect us and let us be led of your Spirit. Let wisdom and understanding and knowledge of your will be ours Lord. Lead us and guide us, give your angels charge over us. Let us yield to your will and your plans for the glory of the Lord Jesus Christ.

Amen

I encourage you to come through this open door before you. You won't be sorry.

Michael

About the Author

Michael Van Vlymen is an author and speaker who ministers and teaches internationally at schools and conferences. Michael's primary passion is to teach that everyone can learn to see in the spirit and learn to walk in the supernatural things of God. Michael is the author of "How to See in the Spirit" a best-seller on the subject of spiritual sight, as well as several other books that encourage believers to live a supernatural lifestyle. Michael, his wife Gordana and family live in Carmel, Indiana and work together to fulfill the plan of God for their lives.

Michael was born again at the age of five, and grew up in the church as the son of pastors and missionaries. Michael was baptized in the Holy Spirit at the age of twenty five and through his own miraculous deliverance began to learn about the supernatural things of God. In 2008 the Lord began to teach him about the spiritual realm and specifically how to see in the spiritual realm. Michael recorded this revelation for several years and then the Lord released him to share this revelation through the writing of his first book. Michael has since gone on to write other books on the supernatural things of God, such as "Translation by Faith" with Dr. Bruce D. Allen of Still Waters International Ministries and "Violent Prayer for your Adult Children."

Other Books by Michael

How To See In The Spirit:
A practical guide on engaging the spirit realm

Having your spiritual eyes opened, and seeing in the spirit realm, is one of the most awesome and profound things you can ever experience as a human being. HOW TO SEE IN THE SPIRIT is a practical guide on engaging the spirit realm.

Translation By Faith
with Dr. Bruce D. Allen
Moving Supernaturally for the Purposes of GOD
(Walking in the Supernatural)

This book has been created to help you not only to learn about Translation by Faith, but also to teach you how to enter in. In it we will cover these topics and more....

Legal Rights * Precedent in the Word * Avoiding Deception * Moving by Faith * Sanctified Imagination * Being Led of the Spirit * Activations and Exercises

Angelic Visitations and Supernatural Encounters:
A Diary of Living in the Supernatural of God

Angelic Visitations and Supernatural Encounters is a record of supernatural events taken from the journal accounts of Michael Van Vlymen, author of How to See in the Spirit. The goal of the author was to show that God's supernatural life is not just for a "chosen few", but for everyday, ordinary people as well. The record of events range from supernatural provision to healings to angelic visitations and more, experienced in normal, everyday living.

Powerful Keys to Spiritual Sight:
Effective Things You Can Do To Open Your Spiritual Eyes

Powerful Keys to Spiritual Sight is a book that explains effective things that you can do to open your spiritual eyes.

Prayer and Fasting ~ Waiting on God ~ Imagination ~ Passion & Desire ~ Atmosphere

These are all things that play a part in the opening of our spiritual eyes. This book seeks to explain in simple and strait-forward terms how to apply all these things in a practical manner so that you know what to do and how to do it.

How To Do Spiritual Warfare
Workbook

This workbook on spiritual warfare is a foundational book that gives solid and practical steps to teach believers exactly how to do the things the Bible tells us to do concerning warfare and dealing with the enemy. The advice and explanations in this book are very specific with scriptural validation so there is no misunderstanding about what to do.

* Example Prayers that cover many different situations
* Explanations about binding and loosing and why it is so effective
* The power of your words and how to speak the word over your life or situation
* How to decree things according to the Word and see them happen
* Why your identity in Christ is so very important
* and much, much more....

SUPERNATURAL TRANSPORTATION

Printed in the USA
CPSIA information can be obtained
at www.ICGtesting.com
LVHW010231041023
760031LV00014B/112